The Moons of Jupiter

Teacher's Guide

Grades 4–9

Skills

Creating/Using Models, Synthesizing, Visualizing, Observing, Explaining, Recording, Measuring, Using a Map, Evaluating Evidence, Inferring, Drawing Conclusions, Creative Designing

Concepts

History of Astronomy, Systems of Planets and Satellites, Revolution and Rotation, Comparing Surface Features, Crater Formation, Geocentric and Heliocentric Models of the Solar System, Vast and Relative Sizes and Distances in Space, Space Settlements

Themes

Systems and Interactions, Stability, Models and Simulations, Patterns of Change, Energy, Scale, Structure

Mathematics Strands

Number, Pattern, Measurement, Functions, Logic

Five to Seven 40- to 50-minute sessions

Debra Sutter
Cary Sneider
Alan Gould
Carolyn Willard
Edna DeVore

WHAT ARE THEMES?

Themes can be seen as major, recurring ideas that provide a framework for the science curriculum. For more on what GEMS means by themes, please see page... vi

D1299914

LHS GEMS

Great Explorations in Math and Science (GEMS)
Lawrence Hall of Science
University of California at Berkeley

Cover
Rose Craig

Illustrations
Lisa Klofkorn

Photographs
Richard Hoyt
Lincoln Bergman

Lawrence Hall of Science, University of California, Berkeley, CA 94720

Chairman: Glenn T. Seaborg
Director: Marian C. Diamond

Publication of *Moons of Jupiter* was made possible by a grant from the McDonnell Douglas Foundation and the McDonnell Douglas Employees Community Fund. The GEMS Project and the Lawrence Hall of Science greatly appreciate this support.

Initial support for the origination and publication of the GEMS series was provided by the A.W. Mellon Foundation and the Carnegie Corporation of New York. Under a grant from the National Science Foundation, GEMS Leader's Workshops have been held across the country. GEMS has also received support from the McDonnell-Douglas Foundation and the McDonnell-Douglas Employees Community Fund, the Hewlett Packard Company Foundation, and the people at Chevron USA. GEMS also gratefully acknowledges the contribution of word processing equipment from Apple Computer, Inc. This support does not imply responsibility for statements or views expressed in publications of the GEMS program. For further information on GEMS leadership opportunities, or to receive a publication brochure and the *GEMS Network News*, please contact GEMS at the address and phone number below.

International Standard Book Number: 0-912511-84-2

COMMENTS WELCOME

Great Explorations in Math and Science (GEMS) is an ongoing curriculum development project. GEMS guides are revised periodically, to incorporate teacher comments and new approaches. We welcome your criticisms, suggestions, helpful hints, and any anecdotes about your experience presenting GEMS activities. Your suggestions will be reviewed each time a GEMS guide is revised. Please send your comments to: GEMS Revisions, c/o Lawrence Hall of Science, University of California, Berkeley, CA 94720. The phone number is (510) 642-7771.

Great Explorations in Math and Science (GEMS) Program

The Lawrence Hall of Science (LHS) is a public science center on the University of California at Berkeley campus. LHS offers a full program of activities for the public, including workshops and classes, exhibits, films, lectures, and special events. LHS is also a center for teacher education and curriculum research and development.

Over the years, LHS staff have developed a multitude of activities, assembly programs, classes, and interactive exhibits. These programs have proven to be successful at the Hall and should be useful to schools, other science centers, museums, and community groups. A number of these guided-discovery activities have been published under the Great Explorations in Math and Science (GEMS) title, after an extensive refinement process that includes classroom testing of trial versions, modifications to ensure the use of easy-to-obtain materials, and carefully written and edited step-by-step instructions and background information to allow presentation by teachers without special background in mathematics or science.

Staff

Glenn T. Seaborg, **Principal Investigator**
Jacqueline Barber, **Director**
Kimi Hosoume, **Assistant Director**
Cary Sneider, **Curriculum Specialist**
Katharine Barrett, Kevin Beals, Ellen Blinderman, Beatrice Boffen, John Erickson, Jaine Kopp, Laura Lowell, Linda Lipner, Debra Sutter, Rebecca Tilley, Laura Tucker, Carolyn Willard, **Staff Development Specialists**
Jan M. Goodman, **Mathematics Consultant**

Cynthia Hom Eaton, **Administrative Coordinator**
Karen Milligan, **Distribution Coordinator**
Lisa Haderlie Baker, **Art Director**
Carol Bevilacqua and Lisa Klofkorn, **Designers**
Lincoln Bergman, **Principal Editor**
Carl Babcock, **Senior Editor**
Kay Fairwell, **Principal Publications Coordinator**
Nancy Kedzierski, Felicia Roston, Vivian Tong, Stephanie Van Meter, **Staff Assistants**

Contributing Authors

Jacqueline Barber
Katharine Barrett
Kevin Beals
Lincoln Bergman
Celia Cuomo
Philip Gonsalves
Jaine Kopp
Linda Lipner
Laura Lowell
Linda De Lucchi

Jean Echols
Jan M. Goodman
Alan Gould
Kimi Hosoume
Susan Jagoda
Larry Malone
Cary I. Sneider
Debra Sutter
Jennifer Meux White
Carolyn Willard

Reviewers

We would like to thank the following educators who reviewed, tested, or coordinated the reviewing of this series of GEMS materials in manuscript and draft form. Their critical comments and recommendations, based on presentation of these activities nationwide, contributed significantly to these GEMS publications. Their participation in the review process does not necessarily imply endorsement of the GEMS program or responsibility for statements or views expressed. Their role in an invaluable one, and their feedback is carefully recorded and integrated as appropriate into the publications. THANK YOU!

ALASKA
Coordinator: **Cynthia Dolmas Curran**

Iditarod Elementary School, Wasilla
   Cynthia Dolmas Curran
   Jana DePriest
   Christina M. Jencks
   Abby Kellner-Rode
   Beverly McPeek

Sherrod Elementary School, Palmer
   Michael Curran
   R. Geoffrey Shank
   Tom Hermon

CALIFORNIA
GEMS Center, Huntington Beach
Coordinator: **Susan Spoeneman**

College View School, Huntington Beach
   Kathy O'Steen
   Robin L. Rouse
   Karen Sandors
   Lisa McCarthy

John Eader School, Huntington Beach
   Jim Atteberry
   Ardis Bucy
   Virginia Ellenson

Issac Sowers Middle School, Huntington Beach
   James E. Martin

San Francisco Bay Area
Coordinator: **Cynthia Eaton**

Bancroft Middle School, San Leandro
   Catherine Heck
   Barbara Kingsley
   Michael Mandel
   Stephen Rutherford

Edward M. Downer Elementary School, San Pablo
   M. Antonieta Franco
   Barbara Kelly
   Linda Searls
   Emily Teale Vogler

Malcolm X Intermediate School, Berkeley
   Candyce Cannon
   Carole Chin
   Denise B. Lebel
   Rudolph Graham
   DeEtte LaRue
   Mahalia Ryba

Marie A. Murphy School, Richmond
   Sally Freese
   Dallas Karahalios
   Susan Jane Kirsch
   Sandra A. Petzoldt
   Versa White

Marin Elementary School, Albany
   Juline Aguilar
   Chris Bowen
   Lois B. Breault
   Nancy Davidson

   Sarah Del Grande
   Marlene Keret
   Juanita Rynerson
   Maggie J. Shepherd
   Sonia Zulpo

Markham Elementary School, Oakland
   Alvin Bettis
   Eleanor Feuille
   Sharon Kerr
   Steven L. Norton
   Patricia Harris Nunley
   Kirsten Pihlaja
   Ruth Quezada

Martin Luther King, Jr. Jr. High
   Phoebe Tanner

Sierra School, El Cerrito
   Laurie Chandler
   Gary DeMoss
   Tanya Grove
   Roselyn Max
   Norman Nemzer
   Martha Salzman
   Diane Simoneau
   Marcia Williams

Sleepy Hollow Elementary School, Orinda
   Lou Caputo
   Marlene Fraser
   Carolyn High
   Janet Howard
   Nancy Medbery
   Kathy Mico-Smith
   Anne H. Morton
   Mary Welte

Walnut Heights Elementary
School, Walnut Creek
   Christl Blumenthal
   Nora Davidson
   Linda Ghysels
   Julie A. Ginocchio
   Sally J. Holcombe
   Thomas F. MacLean
   Elizabeth O'Brien
   Gail F. Puleo

Willard Junior High School,
Berkeley
   Vana James
   Linda Taylor-White
   Katherine Evans

GEORGIA
Coordinator: **Yonnie Carol**
Pope

Dodgen Middle School,
Marietta
   Linda W. Curtis
   Joan B. Jackson
   Marilyn Pope
   Wanda Richardson

Mountain View Elementary
School, Marietta
   Cathy Howell
   Diane Pine Miller
   Janie E. Stokes
   Elaine S. Toney

NEW YORK
Coordinator: **Stanley J.**
Wegrzynowski

Dr. Charles R. Drew Science
Magnet, Buffalo
   Mary Jean Syrek
   Renée C. Johnson
   Ruth Kresser
   Jane Wenner Metzger
   Sharon Pikul

Lorraine Academy, Buffalo
   Francine R. LoGrippo
   Clintonia R. Graves
   Albert Gurgol
   Nancy B. Kryszczuk
   Laura P. Parks

OREGON
Coordinator: **Anne Kennedy**

Myers Elementary School,
Salem
   Cheryl A. Ward
   Carol Nivens
   Kent C. Norris
   Tami Socolofsky

Terrebonne Elementary School,
Terrebonne
   Francy Stillwell
   Elizabeth M. Naidis
   Carol Selle
   Julie Wellette

Wallowa Elementary School,
Wallowa
   Sherry Carman
   Jennifer K. Isley
   Neil A. Miller
   Warren J. Wilson

PENNSYVANIA
Coordinator: **Greg Calvetti**

Aliquippa Elementary School,
Aliquippa
   Karen Levitt
   Lorraine McKinin
   Ted Zeljak

Duquesne Elementary School,
Duquesne
   Tim Kamauf
   Mike Vranesivic
   Elizabeth A. West

Gateway Upper Elementary
School, Monroeville
   Paul A. Bigos
   Reed Douglas Hankinson
   Barbara B. Messina
   Barbara Platz
   William Wilshire

Ramsey Elementary School,
Monroeville
   Faye Ward

WASHINGTON
Coordinator: **David Kennedy**

Blue Ridge Elementary School,
Walla Walla
   Peggy Harris Willcuts

Prospect Point School, Walla
Walla
   Alice R. MacDonald
   Nancy Ann McCorkle

MORE ON THEMES

The word "themes" is used in many different ways in both ordinary usage and in educational circles. In the GEMS series, themes are seen as key recurring ideas that cut across all the scientific disciplines. Themes are bigger than facts, concepts, or theories. They link various theories from many disciplines. They have also been described as "the sap that runs through the curriculum," to convey the sense that they permeate through and arise from the curriculum. By listing the themes that run through a particular GEMS unit on the title page, we hope to assist you in seeing where the unit fits into the "big picture" of science, and how the unit connects to other GEMS units. The theme "Patterns of Change," for example, suggests that the unit or some important part of it exemplifies larger scientific ideas about why, how, and in what ways change takes place, whether it be a chemical reaction or a caterpillar becoming a butterfly. GEMS has selected 10 major themes:

Systems & Interactions	Scale
Models & Simulations	Structure
Stability	Energy
Patterns of Change	Matter
Evolution	Diversity & Unity

If you are interested in thinking more about themes and the thematic approach to teaching and constructing curriculum, you may wish to obtain a copy of our handbook, *To Build A House: GEMS and the Thematic Approach to Teaching Science.* For more information and an order brochure, write or call GEMS, Lawrence Hall of Science, University of California, Berkeley, CA 94720. (510) 642-7771. **Thanks for your interest in GEMS!**

Contents

Acknowledgments

The activities in this unit have been presented in many classes at the Lawrence Hall of Science (LHS) over the past decade. Many instructors have contributed to their improvement. Inspiration for the various activities included in this guide came from the following sources:

Activity 1: Tracking Jupiter's Moons, was developed by Cary Sneider. It was inspired by the beautiful curvilinear graphs pictured in issues of *Sky and Telescope* magazine, which show the positions of Jupiter's moons during the month. The activity was published in *The Planetarian*, vol. 15, no. 3, 3rd Quarter, 1986, and in the LHS series, Planetarium Activities for Student Success (PASS), Volume 2, *Planetarium Activities for Schools*, 1990. The Modeling Moon Phases "Going Further" activity is based on an activity independently developed by Dennis Schatz and Larry Moscotti in the 1970s, and published in *Planetarium Educator's Workshop Guide*, IPS Special Report #10, by Alan Friedman, Dennis Schatz, Larry Lowery, Steven Pulos, and Cary Sneider, International Planetarium Society, 1980. It is one of the activities in the GEMS guide *Earth, Moon, and Stars*.

Activity 2: Experimenting With Craters, was developed by Alan Gould with additional refinements by the other authors of this guide. It is published in the LHS series Planetarium Activities for Student Success (PASS), Volume 7, *Moons of the Solar System*, 1990. Activity 3: A Scale Model of the Jupiter System, was inspired by many scale model activities, including an especially interesting presentation by Phillip Sadler at the National Science Teachers' Association (NSTA) National Convention in St. Louis, Missouri, in 1988.

Activity 4: A Grand Tour of the Jupiter System, was adapted from the LHS planetarium program entitled "Moons of the Solar System." The idea of comparing each of the moons with a map of the United States was inspired by "Worlds In Comparison," a slide set created and distributed by the Astronomical Society of the Pacific. Activity 5: Creating Moon Settlements, is based on a class for the LHS after-school and summer programs, developed by Alan Gould, and entitled "Space Settlements."

The teachers who assisted in our testing process are listed at the front of this guide. Our special thanks to them and their enthusiastic students. GEMS Administrative Coordinator Cynthia Eaton coordinated the national testing, Stephanie Van Meter was instrumental in putting the local and national teacher kits together, and Vivian Tong assisted in arranging duplication of the slides. Thanks as well to Audre Newman for her help with illustrations in the "Background for Teachers" section.

The three poems in this guide are by the GEMS Principal Editor Lincoln Bergman.

1993: Jan. 5 a

Introduction

Many teachers remember the exciting discoveries made by the two Voyager spacecraft as they sped through the Jupiter System in 1979. Voyagers 1 and 2 sent back amazing images to Earth—the first-ever close-up photos of Jupiter and its four major moons. Yet to most of our students, this is ancient history! These GEMS *Moons of Jupiter* activities rekindle the excitement of those early days of space exploration, which made people realize, as never before, that our familiar "Luna" is not the only interesting moon in the solar system. Over 50 "worlds" were surveyed by spacecraft in the 1970s and 1980s!

The first activity, "Tracking Jupiter's Moons," brings us back to the year 1609, when Galileo Galilei first turned a telescope on the heavens, and saw four curious "stars" in a straight line in the vicinity of Jupiter. After observing these tiny points of light for many nights, a flash of insight led him to conclude that he was seeing *moons* around another world. Even today, we call these four large moons of Jupiter, the "Galilean Satellites." Your students will recreate this important moment in the history of science as they track the moons of Jupiter and calculate their periods of revolution, just as Galileo did.

Beginning our study of moon surfaces by looking at our own Luna, the most striking feature is the tremendous number of circular depressions known as "craters." As we look at the craters we see some very interesting aspects—rays that seem to be sprayed out from the crater's center, circles of mountains around the larger craters, and tall mountains in the centers of some of them. In Activity 2, your students build a model of the Moon's pulverized surface and drop "meteors" on it to see what will happen. Surprisingly, they can create some features that are very much like those actually seen on Earth's Moon! Will we see such features on Jupiter's moons as well?

Jupiter's moons are not only huge, they are separated by vast distances that make their huge bulk seem like tiny specks in the void. Communicating the scale of the Jupiter system is the great challenge of Activity 3. Using a classroom scale model of the Earth-Moon system as a basis of comparison, your students mark the distances within the Jupiter system on the schoolyard.

Now for a "grand tour" of these four bizarre worlds of rock, ice, craters, mountains, and even active volcanoes! In Activity 4, your students tour the Jupiter System through slides and draw their own pictures to illustrate the volcanic, pock-marked, pizza-like face of Io; the smooth, finely cracked surface of the giant "cueball" known as Europa; the grooved, icy mountains of the largest moon in the solar system, Ganymede; the gigantic crater called Valhalla on Callisto.

Perhaps the most enjoyable activity of all for the students is the very creative final session in which they bring all that they have learned during the unit to bear on the challenge of designing and building a model of a space settlement on one of the moons of Jupiter. Using bits and pieces of scrap paper and plastic, your students may imagine pressurized buildings, scientific observatories, and comfortable quarters for crewmembers who may spend years in the freezing conditions of Callisto, or the dangerous volcanic environment of Io. They will imagine what life might be like there, how they will obtain food and water, and what amazing sights they might see.

In all of these activities, your students create and use models of various kinds. They start with a simple record of their observations in the Tracking Jupiter's Moons activity, and imagine that the dots they see are moons circling the giant planet, Jupiter. Both meteors and the moon's surface are modeled in the crater experiments. To gain an idea of the vastness of the Jupiter system, the students compare that system to our Earth-moon system using scale models. In the Grand Tour of the Jupiter System, the students learn how scientists have examined photographic evidence gathered by the Voyager spacecraft, and made inferences concerning what might have caused the various surface features and markings. Such inferences are visualized as a model of the Moon that would explain the observed markings. And finally, they use models very creatively to design settlements that could house the first human explorers in the Jupiter System.

Making and using models of various types is one of the most important processes used by scientists and engineers to explore the space environment. It is also one of the most important components of science and technology in general. Emphasis in this unit is on developing the students' abilities to make and use a wide variety of models so they can answer their own questions, rather than providing them with a lot of information that they are expected to memorize.

Even though emphasis is on the process of making and using models, teachers may also wish to learn as much as possible about the Jupiter System, so they may be better prepared when their students ask questions. Therefore, we have included a "Background for Teachers" section, which contains a brief overview of some of the scientific findings about the Jupiter system and the Solar System. There is also a "Resources" section for those who wish to go further in learning about Jupiter and its satellites, including information on when Jupiter is visible in the sky, as well as additional resources for use in the classroom.

Summary Outlines are provided for your convenience to help you guide your students through these activities. Data sheets appear at the end of each activity in which they are needed. Additional, removable copies of student data sheets are included at the back of the guide.

If you have purchased this book from the Lawrence Hall of Science, you will also have received a set of slides **required** for the activities. The slides provide large, colorful images, revealing the moons of Jupiter in all their beauty and splendor. If for some reason you do not have the slides, an address is given in the "Getting Ready" section of the first activity, so you can purchase the set.

One final thought—it is sometimes easy to forget that Jupiter and its moons really exist. They are not simply pretty pictures in a textbook or in a series of slides. Anyone (including you and your students) can go outdoors on many nights of the year, and look up to see what appears to be a very bright, untwinkling star. Binoculars will reveal three or four tiny bright dots nearby, all in a line. Then you could marvel, along with Galileo, "Hmmmm....I wonder what they can be." And wonder, as Emerson once said, is the seed of science.

Time Frame

The preparation times **estimated** below include time to set up the classroom and prepare special materials. They do not include time to read through the guide or to shop for materials. Classroom activity time will vary greatly depending on your particular group of students, as well as your own needs and preferences.

Activity 1: Tracking Jupiter's Moons

Preparation   20–30 minutes
Class activity 45 minutes

Activity 2: Experimenting With Craters

Preparation   60 minutes
Class activity 60 minutes (data collection may extend this time)
Cleanup   30 minutes

Activity 3: A Scale Model of the Jupiter System

Preparation   45–60 minutes
Class activity 60 minutes

Activity 4: A Grand Tour of the Jupiter System

Preparation   45 minutes
Class activity one or two 45–60 minute sessions

Activity 5: Creating Moon Settlements

Preparation   45-60 minutes
Class activity one to three 45–60 minute sessions

IMPORTANT NOTE: Activity 5 requires quite a bit of material for the teacher to collect and/or for the students to bring from home. It is suggested that you begin collecting this material when you start the unit. See the "doo-dad" section, page 53.

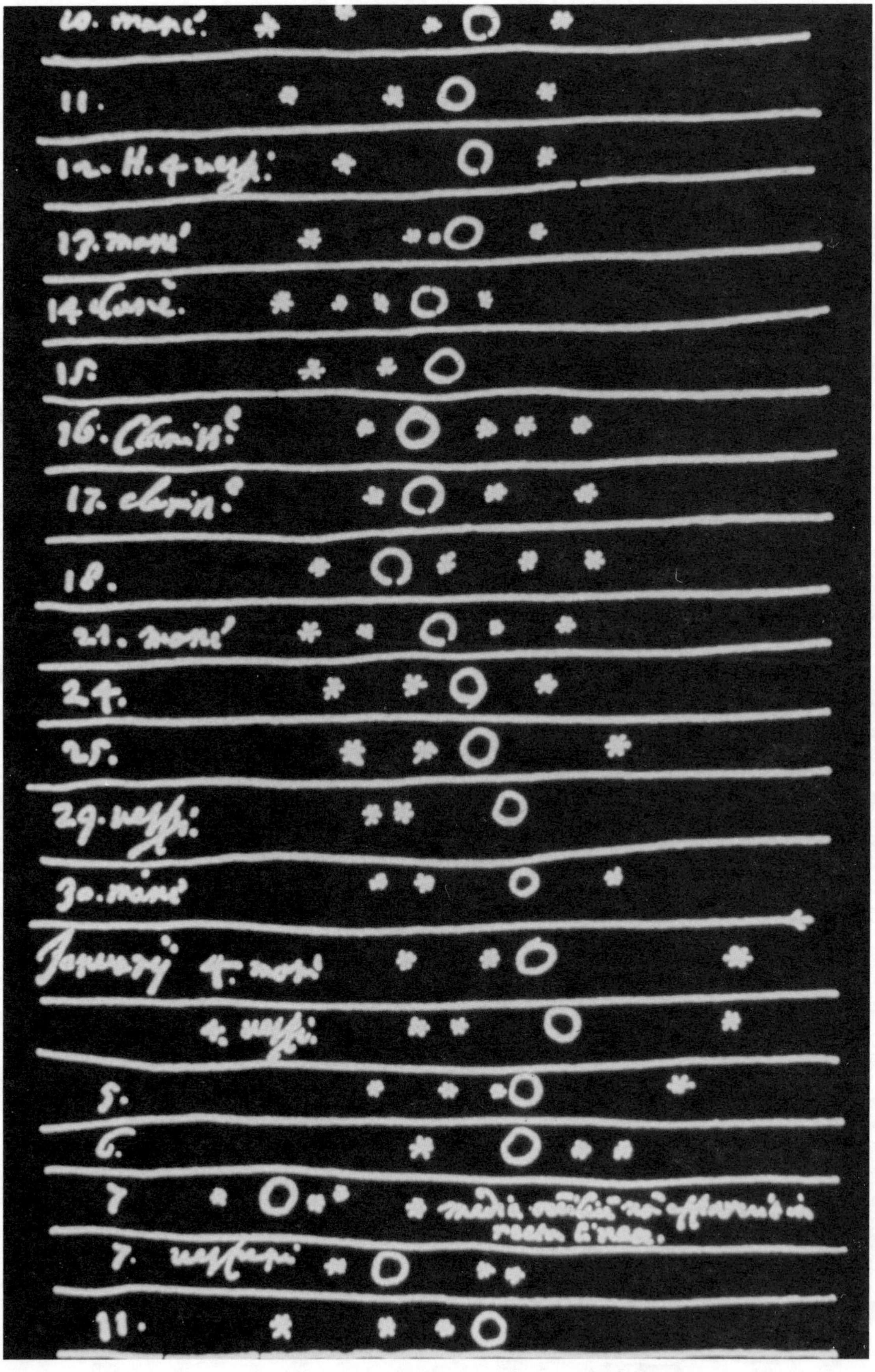
10. mane.
11.
12. H. 4 vesp:
13. mane
14
15:
16.
17.
18.
21. mane
24.
25.
29. vesp:
30. mane
Januarij 4. mane
4. vesp:
5.
6.
7
7. vespere
11.

1993: Jan. 6 b

Activity 1: Tracking Jupiter's Moons

Overview

In 1609, when Galileo pointed a telescope at the planet Jupiter, he was amazed to see four bright points of light near the planet. Could they be moons of Jupiter?

In this activity, your classroom astronomers observe a series of slides of Jupiter and its moons, over a period of nine nights. Excitement will mount as students record their observations on each "night," notice how the moons change position in relation to Jupiter, and determine how long it takes each moon to make one complete revolution around the planet.

What You Need

For the class:

❑ Slides #1–#11. (One set of slides is included with this book. Additional sets are available for purchase from the GEMS Project c/o Lawrence Hall of Science, University of California, Berkeley, CA 94720.)

❑ 2 balls, one much larger than the other, for example: a softball and a ping pong ball; or a tennis ball and a marble.

❑ 1 slide projector and screen

❑ (optional) 1 overhead projector

❑ (optional) 1 set of overhead projector pens

❑ (optional) 4 transparencies of the data sheet (master on page 16)

For each student:

❑ 1 copy of "Tracking Jupiter's Moons Data Sheet" (page 16)

❑ 1 pencil

Slides are labeled so that, as you place them into the slide tray, the label will be on top and readable, as shown above. When this is done, the slide orientation when projected will be correct.

Getting Ready

1. Make one copy of the data sheet for each student. (Master included on page 16.)

2. Plan how you will divide the class into teams for the activity. Each team will observe one moon. Members of each team will need to be seated close enough together to compare notes. The number and size of the teams may vary, as long as you have at least one team (of from four to eight students) to observe each of the four moons. In a class of 32 students, for example, you may decide to have a group of eight students observe each of the four moons. Or you may decide to have eight teams of four, and assign two teams to observe each moon.

3. Set up the slide projector and have slides #1 through #11 ready for viewing. (A complete list of the slides appears on page 88.) Prepare to darken the room.

4. (Optional) Make 4 transparencies of the data sheet, using a photocopy process so they are all the same.

Slide 12 – "Earth's Moon, Luna"

Optional: Some teachers like to project the slide of the Earth's Moon here. (It is also used later, in Session 2.)

GO!

Galileo and His Telescope

1. Explain that an Italian scientist named Galileo Galilei, who lived about 400 years ago, was the first person to study the sky using a telescope. (He did not, however, *invent* the telescope.) Usually, we just refer to him by his first name, Galileo. Ask your students, "If you had just built a telescope, what would you want to look at?" Accept all answers.

2. If no one mentions it, say that Galileo looked at planets, too. Ask, "What does a planet look like in the night sky, using just your unaided eyes?" [It looks much like a star.] Ask your students, "What would a planet look like through a telescope?" After generating a few ideas, darken the room as appropriate and **show the first slide: Jupiter with four white moons.** Tell your students that Galileo might have seen something similar to this. Ask them to guess which planet it is.

Slide 1 – "Jupiter and four moons"

3. Explain that when Galileo observed Jupiter, he was the first person to see that planets are ball-shaped. He also noticed four star-like points of light lined up on either side of the planet. He noted that night after night, the four star-like objects appeared in different places. Say that this was very unusual since other stars never change position in relation to one another.

A planet is less "twinkly" than a star and some of your students may mention this. It is a subtle difference and often hard to perceive. Through a telescope, Jupiter looks like a disc, while the stars still look like points because, even though they are much larger in size than Jupiter, they are much farther away.

4. Tell your students that Galileo also noticed that, as Jupiter moved across the sky, these "star-like" objects moved with it. Ask the class what these objects could be. [They are Jupiter's four largest moons.]

5. Explain that during the next activity the class will keep records, just as Galileo did, see the same things he saw, and try to figure out what might be happening.

Tracking Jupiter's Moons

1. Hand out data sheets to all the students and have them get their pencils ready.

2. Explain to the students that they will watch Jupiter and its moons as they might appear for nine nights. Point out that the moons on this slide have been colored so that it is easier to tell them apart.

3. **Advance to the next slide, "*Night 1*."** Also point out the numbers that indicate the distance from Jupiter in *millions* of miles. Explain that the number 1 is about 1 million miles to the "right" of the planet. To show that a moon is to the "left" of the planet, we have used minus numbers, so minus 2 represents 2 million miles "left" of Jupiter.

4. Divide the class into teams. Ask the students to imagine that they are teams of astronomers, and assign each of the teams to observe *one* of the moons. Ask them to write, at the top of their data sheets, the color of the moon that they will observe.

5. Tell the students to find the position of their moon in relation to Jupiter in the slide for *Night 1*. Ask them to place an "X" on their data sheet on the "Night 1" line to show the position of their moon as they see it in relation to Jupiter.

6. Have teams compare data and help other members within their group. Before going on with the slides, go around the classroom and check to see that each student understands how to record the position of his or her moon.

7. Tell your students that you will use the slide projector as a "time machine" and let an entire day go by until you arrive at Night 2. You may want to turn the room lights on for daylight, then off again for night.

Slide 2 – "Night 1"

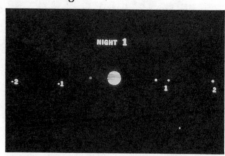

Optional: You may want to demonstrate recording Night 1 with an overhead projector and a transparency of the data sheet.

Slide 3 – "Night 2"

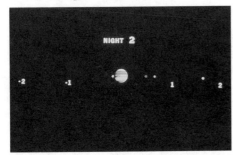

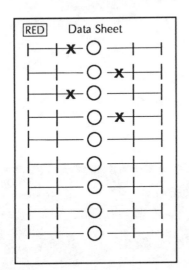

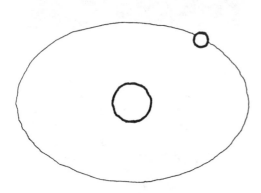

TOP VIEW

SIDE VIEW

8. **Advance slide to *Night 2*.** Have students locate their moon and mark its position with respect to Jupiter on the appropriate line of their data sheets. Ask, "Where is your moon on Night 2?"

9. Check to see if the students have marked the position of their moon on the second line. (Some may put all of the X's on the same line. **Be sure they understand that each observation must be recorded on the next lower line.**) Continue for each night, advancing the slides as needed, going a little faster as the students improve their recording abilities.

10. After three or four nights, have them predict where their moon will be on the next night. (They may want to place a light dot on the appropriate line.) Then, continue until the students have observed Jupiter's moons for all nine nights.

Summarizing the Data

1. With the slide of *Night 9*, the students will have completed their data sheets. Now is the time to summarize the observations. Turn off the slide projector and turn room lights on. **(Your students will need at least 15 minutes to summarize their observations. If the time left in the class period is too short, you may want to postpone the summary and discussion for another time.)**

2. Tell your students to draw a line on their data sheets connecting the positions of their moon as it changed from night to night. (Each of the four moons will generate a different "zigzag" pattern as students connect the X's.)

3. Have students compare data with their teammates who observed the same moon. Give them time to discuss any differences in their observations. If students request it, you may show the slides again so they can resolve disagreements. (Although an astronomer would of course not be able to see the same nights over again, she would be able to keep watching as the moons continued their motions on subsequent nights.)

4. Ask the students to describe *what might be happening* that would explain why their moons seemed to change position each night. [The moon is circling around the planet.]

5. Model Jupiter and one of its moons using a large and small ball. By moving the small ball in a *vertical* circle around the large ball, show how we can see the moon going in a circle, or

1993: Jan. 7 b

orbit, around Jupiter, if we view the planet from above. Then demonstrate how, when viewed from the side, the moon's orbit *appears* to go from one side of Jupiter to the other. Thus, from the side, the moons appear in different positions on either side of the planet, just as they appeared on the slides.

6. Ask, "How can we figure out how long it takes for a moon to go around Jupiter once?" Get ideas from the students. If they need help visualizing the problem, you might want them to imagine a car going around a race track. When the car gets back to the place it started from, that means it has gone around the track once.

7. Tell the students who observed the same moon to work together to determine from their data how long it takes their moon to go around Jupiter once. Have them count the spaces between the lines to tell how many days have gone by since Night #1.

8. Go from group to group to assist if necessary. Guide students who are having difficulty as follows:

a. Locate the position your moon started from along the line for *Night 1* (you can place your pencil on the mark).

b. Look down the page to find the night when it was in nearly the same position.

c. Since one day goes by between each line, you can determine the number of days it took your moon to go around Jupiter, by counting the spaces between the lines.

9. Circulate, offering suggestions to the teams as they work. Teams who are determining the white moon's orbital period may need help, since that moon did not return to its starting position, but went to the other side of Jupiter between nights one and nine. The students may conclude that the white moon takes 18 days to orbit once. Ask them to count the days between nights 1 and 9. [8 days] How many more days will go by before the moon returns to its starting position? [8 days, for a total of 16 days]

10. (Optional) Have students who finish early in each group of students trace their data sheet onto a separate overhead transparency. Use the same color coding of the moons that was used on the slides. (Use a black marker for the white moon.)

You may wish to add that, with powerful modern telescopes, astronomers can sometimes see one of the moons disappear behind Jupiter. (This is called an occultation.) On other occasions, they can see the shadow of a moon on Jupiter as it passes between the Sun and Jupiter. When a moon goes in front of Jupiter, that is called a "transit."

Slide 4

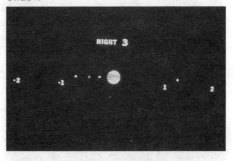

Slide 5

Slide 6

Slide 7

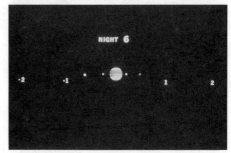

You may want to remind the students that, in reality, all four moons look white in a telescope.

Slide 8

Slide 9

Slide 10

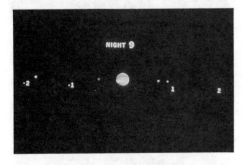

Slide 11

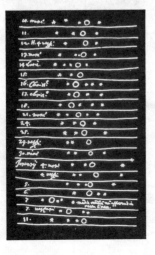

Discussing the Results

1. For each of the four moons, have one student hold up her data sheet (or show it on the overhead projector) and reveal the number of days it took for that group's moon to orbit Jupiter. Accept all group results, along with any discussion and explanations. Record the students' results along with the color and name of each of the moons on the chalkboard or overhead:

RED moon	Io (pronounced EYE-oh)	?	days
YELLOW moon	Europa (your-OH-pah)	?	days
BLUE moon	Ganymede (GAN-ee-meed)	?	days
WHITE moon	Callisto (Cah-LIST-oh)	?	days

2. Students' results may vary somewhat, depending on their observing and recording skills and the method they used to count the nights. It is not important that your students' results exactly match those of today's scientists. Tell your class that modern astronomers have found results much like theirs: Red moon, Io—2 days, Yellow moon, Europa—4 days, Blue moon, Ganymede—7 days, and White moon, Callisto—16 days.

3. Ask students if they notice a relationship between the time it takes a moon to orbit Jupiter and the moon's distance from the planet?" [The farther away it is, the more time one orbit takes.]

4. Turn on the slide projector and show Slide #11, Galileo's Notes. Tell your students that although Galileo wrote in Italian, they might be able to understand a page out of his notebook now. He took notes similar to theirs! Have your students identify the symbols and notations they recognize. (They should be able to identify a column of dates, Jupiter as a circle, and the moons as "stars" on either side.)

5. Ask the students why they think Galileo's discovery of the moons of Jupiter was so important, almost four hundred years ago.

6. Explain that in Galileo's day, most people believed that the Sun, Moon, planets, and stars revolved around the Earth. That made a lot of sense because the Earth certainly doesn't feel like it is moving! Fifty years *before* Galileo, an astronomer named Copernicus proposed that the Earth and other planets went around the Sun; only the Moon circled the Earth. How do you think Galileo may have used his discovery of Jupiter's moons when talking about Copernicus' theory with other scientists?

1993: Jan. 8 a

[Galileo showed that not all celestial bodies went around Earth. Also, the Jupiter system was a model for the solar system. Moons go around Jupiter just as the planets go around the Sun.]

Going Further (for Activity 1)

1. If you made four overhead transparencies of the data sheets, and had four students trace the data from the four different moons onto them (using different colored pens if possible) you can combine them as follows: Stack the completed transparencies so they are carefully lined up. Punch two holes at the top or side, so paper fasteners can be used to line them up quickly. Stack the four transparencies together, one at a time, on the overhead projector as the students watch. Ask questions about the combined graph such as:

> How will Jupiter's moons appear on night 3? 4? 5?

> On what night does the white moon go from one side of Jupiter to the other?

> On what night will most of the moons be on the left side of Jupiter?

> On what night will we see two moons on each side of Jupiter?

2. Several magazines, such as *Astronomy* and *Sky & Telescope* have a monthly graph of Jupiter's moons that looks very much like the combined graph above. Show this graph to your students, and ask them further questions, such as:

> How many nights are represented on this graph? (one month, usually 30 or 31 nights)

> What does the column down the middle stand for? (Jupiter)

> How many moons are plotted on the graph? (four)

> How will the moons appear on the 15th (or other interesting date) of the month?

> How are the moons labeled on this graph? (In *Sky & Telescope* they are labeled by Roman numerals.) Which moon corresponds to which Roman numeral? When will moon III be behind Jupiter?

For older students, you may want to point out that the order of the four moons, in terms of distance from Jupiter, is Io, Europa, Ganymede, Callisto. Ask, "Why, if Callisto is the farthest from Jupiter, does it appears to be closer to Jupiter than Europa on Night 5?" [Answering this question reinforces the concepts demonstrated by the small and large ball involving side and top views of a moon's orbit.]

It is important to note that if you are observing the real Jupiter, you often see just three moons. Notice that this is true in Galileo's record. Why is this? [Sometimes one or more moon(s) are in front of or behind Jupiter, and cannot be seen.]

See the "Background for Teachers" section for more information on the early astronomers and their theories.

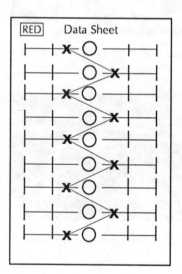

Which moon orbits Jupiter the largest number of times? The smallest number of times?

Can you find a date when three of the moons will be found on the one side of Jupiter? On the other side?

3. **Galileo.** Have your students read more about Galileo's life, and the trouble he got into because of his defense of Copernicus's theory. Plays by Bertolt Brecht and others have been written about Galileo's life. Your students might want to put on such a play, or make up one of their own.

4. **"Wandering Stars."** Use a sheet of aluminum foil and an overhead projector to model how stars appear fixed in relation to each other, while planets seem to "wander" among the stars.

a. In a sheet of aluminum foil, punch holes for stars with the sharp point of a pencil to make the constellation Leo, as shown at left. (Make the same pattern of stars as in the constellation but enlarge it.) The star Regulus is larger than the other stars. Make **three additional holes** to show the locations of a planet at three different times as it moves through the constellation. **The three holes showing the planet should be as large as the smaller stars.** Cover two of the planet holes with Post-its™ or bits of paper.

b. Project the image of the constellation Leo with only one of the planet positions visible. Explain that one of these "stars" is not really a star, but a planet. Ask the students which one they think is the planet and why. [Often, students will select Regulus, the brightest star. Ask for several opinions.]

c. Tell the students that one way to find out which are planets and which are stars is to observe the sky for several nights, and to watch for changes.

d. Turn off the overhead projector. Using a "post-it" or scrap of paper, *cover up* the first planet position and *uncover* the next planet position. Tell your students that this is how the sky might look after several days have passed. Do they notice a difference? Can they identify which one is the planet now? Can they predict where the planet will be after several more nights have passed?

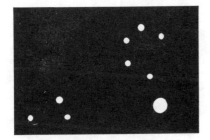

Constellation Leo

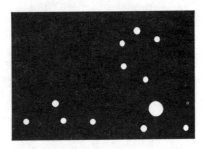

Constellation Leo with 3 planet locations

e. Repeat Step d. once again, this time leaving only the third "planet hole" uncovered. Ask your students if they can identify the planet now. [Nearly all will identify the star that moves this time.]

f. Explain that thousands of years ago, people noticed that nearly all stars stayed in the same patterns as they moved across the sky during the night, so they called them "fixed stars." But certain stars seemed to slowly wander among the fixed stars. Ancient Greeks called these "wandering stars" *planetes*, which is the origin of our word, *planet*. Ask students why they think planets seem to wander among the stars. [They orbit the Sun.]

5. **Arrange an outing** on a night when Jupiter will be visible in the night sky. Using binoculars or telescopes, students will be able to see Jupiter and some of its four largest moons. Contact your local amateur astronomy club to see if they might help your students have a "star party" when Jupiter is visible.

For more information on viewing Jupiter, see the "Jupiter Visibility Guide" on page 89.

6. **Modeling Moon Phases**: If you happened to live on the planet Jupiter and looked up into the beautiful night sky, what might its moons look like? Imagine seeing the full moon of Io rising as the crescent-shaped Ganymede begins to set. To a "Jupiterian," the Galilean satellites would appear to go through the same phases as does our own Moon from Earth. To help your students explore moon phases, we recommend "Modeling Moon Phases and Eclipses" from the GEMS unit, *Earth, Moon, and Stars*. Please see that guide for complete instructions. The simple model developed in this earlier GEMS unit to explain our Moon's monthly cycle of phases can be applied to the more complex Jupiter system.

Adapting the procedures of that model, have students work in teams of three. One student plays the role of "Jupiter" while the other two students each hold up two of Jupiter's four moons. The room is darkened and one bright bulb is turned on, to be the "Sun." Jupiter slowly turns and the phases of its four "moons" can then be observed. The students holding the moons can then move around a little further in their orbits and stop so "Jupiter" can again turn on its axis and students can see how the phases have changed.

7. **Make a flip book** "movie" of Callisto and Ganymede revolving around Jupiter! Make a copy of page 101 for each student. Have them follow the directions on the page. And, don't forget to flip pages 1–93 in this guide for your very own Callisto/Ganymede "teacher's flip book "movie!

Name_____

Color code
of your moon:_____

TRACKING JUPITER'S MOONS

Night 1

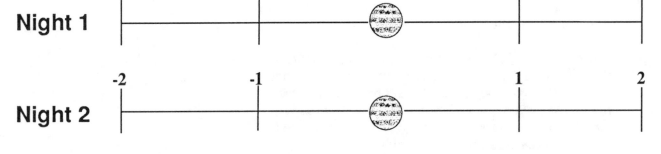

-2   -1   1   2

Night 2

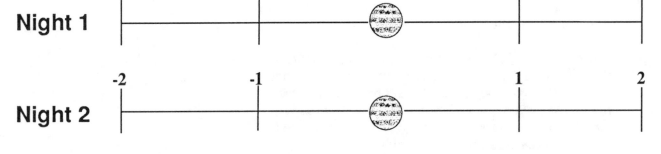

-2   -1   1   2

Night 3

-2   -1   1   2

Night 4

-2   -1   1   2

Night 5

-2   -1   1   2

Night 6

-2   -1   1   2

Night 7

-2   -1   1   2

Night 8

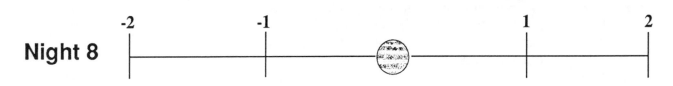

-2   -1   1   2

Night 9

-2   -1   1   2

Lawrence Hall of Science
© 1993 by the Regents of the University of California

The MOONS of JUPITER

Orange planet of such majesty,

The biggest in our family.

Three Earths in fact could snugly squeeze

Inside your red spot's boundaries.

Your many moons, as all agree,

Have wonders and diversity.

Eruptions roar or ice cracks cold,

So many mysteries they hold.

The more we explore, the less we are stupider—

So let's go visit the moons of Jupiter!

Activity 2: Experimenting With Craters

Overview

Craters are among the most fascinating features of many moons. In this activity, your students experiment to find out more about what causes the various features of impact craters, including the rim of mountains around the edge, and the streaks or rays that fan out from large craters. What they learn in this activity about our own Moon, Luna, they can later compare and contrast to what they find out about the moons of Jupiter.

What You Need

For the class:
❑ Slide set including:
  # 12   Earth's Moon
  # 13   Close-Up of Large Crater
❑ 1 slide projector and screen
❑ 1 or more brooms or whisk brooms to clean up spills
❑ 1 pair of scissors or a paper cutter (to cut the centimeter rulers off the student data sheets)
❑ one container instant chocolate milk powder. (Note: Real cocoa has also been used, but it tends to clump and to over-darken the flour too quickly.)
❑ three or four 5-pound packages of white flour

For each team of 4 students:
❑ 1 shallow basin (to be filled with about 3 to 5 inches of flour) Examples: a dishpan, a heavy aluminum roasting pan, or cardboard box. To be sure to have enough, you may want to ask a student from each group to bring in a dishpan from home for the day of the activity. They don't all have to be the same size.
❑ 1 cup or small plastic container (to be filled about one-third full with powdered instant chocolate milk mix)
❑ an old newspaper
❑ three rocks: small, medium, and large
  with diameters **about:** .5 cm ($\frac{1}{4}$ inch), 2 cm ($\frac{3}{4}$ inch) and
  4 cm (about $1\frac{1}{2}$ inches)
❑ 1 spoon (plastic or metal)

For each student:
❑ 1 pencil
❑ 1 "Craters" activity sheet (master on page 28)

Getting Ready

1. Before the day of the activity, collect and sort the rocks needed for all the groups.

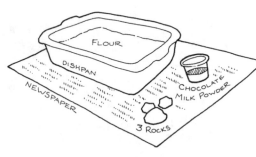

2. Make one copy of the "Craters" data sheet for each student (master on page 28). With scissors or a paper cutter, cut the centimeter rulers from the bottom of the data sheets.

3. Assemble sets of materials for the teams: newspaper, a dishpan filled with flour 3 to 5 inches deep, a cup about one-third full of instant chocolate milk mix, and three different-sized rocks. Have data sheets, paper rulers, and pencils handy, but separate from the other materials. Keep one set of all the materials handy near the place where you will demonstrate the activity.

4. Try the cratering activity yourself so you will know what to expect. Weather permitting, some teachers prefer to do this activity outside for more space and less cleanup. Decide whether your students will do the activity indoors or outdoors.

5. In these activities, there is first free exploration and then more focused cratering experiments that use data sheets. You will need to get the attention of your whole class for instructions before they begin both the free exploration and the more focused experiments. We recommend gathering your class away from the materials for both of these introductions. Some classrooms do not have enough space for students to leave the materials and gather for the second set of instructions. If this is the case, consider explaining all parts of the activity before distributing any of the materials. Read over the lesson, and decide if you'll need to modify your introduction in this way.

6. Set up the slide projector and have slides #12 and #13 ready for viewing (front side of the Moon and close-up of a crater). Prepare to darken the room by drawing curtains or shades.

1993: Jan. 10 a

Meteors and Craters

Slide 12

1. Tell the class that the name of Earth's Moon is *Luna*. Encourage students to begin thinking about Luna by asking them to imagine landing on the Moon's surface.

What do you imagine the surface of our Moon is like?

What would it feel like to be walking on Luna?

What would you see around you?

2. Dim the room lights and turn on the slide projector. Show slide #12, the image of the Earth's Moon. (This is the side of the Moon that always faces Earth.) Tell them that this is how our Moon would look if viewed through a small telescope.

3. Ask, "What do you see on the Moon's surface?" Accept their responses (for example, light areas, dark areas, craters etc.). If somebody mentions craters, have them point out an example of one for the class. If craters are not mentioned, point out a large one and identify it as a crater. Explain that craters are big "dents" or holes in the Moon's surface. Do not go into detail about other surface features at this time.

4. Turn on the room lights and turn off the slide projector. Ask, "What causes craters on the Moon?" [Most students will have an answer for this question and may use terms such as: meteors, asteroids, big rocks, comets, etc.]

5. Ask students if they know what a *meteor* is. [A rock from space falling toward a planet or moon.]

6. Ask your students if there are craters on the Earth. If anybody has visited a crater site, have them share their experience with the class. Explain that the Earth has many craters. Some were caused by volcanoes. Others, called *impact craters*, were made by meteorites. Ask, "Why do we see very few impact craters on the Earth?" [The Earth has rain and wind which erode away the evidence of most craters.]

7. Explain that Earth's atmosphere prevents small meteors from reaching the surface, because when a meteor falls toward a planet with an atmosphere, it "rubs" against the air.

8. Have your students rub their hands together quickly for about ten seconds (counting "one-thousand-one, one-thousand-two," etc.) Ask what they feel. [Heat.] Tell them that if they could rub fast enough they would create enough friction to light a fire.

Between the years 1969 and 1972, six spacecraft from the United States visited the Moon, enabling twelve people to walk on its surface. They had to wear space suits, which create Earth conditions in unearthly places. The space suits carry air to breathe, air pressure that keeps the blood from boiling, and protects the wearer from burning in the sunlight or freezing in the shade. Since the Moon's gravity is one-sixth Earth's gravity, the astronauts are able to jump higher than on Earth. Since they also fall more slowly, they seem to move in slow motion.

*Since the terms are often confusing, you may wish to explain that a **meteoroid** is a rock in space; a **meteor** is the same rock falling through the Earth's atmosphere, creating a streak of light (sometimes also called a "shooting star"). Fragments of meteors that survive the fiery trip through the atmosphere and land on the surface are called **meteorites**. However, it is not important for students to memorize these terms.*

Activity 2 **21**

9. Explain that, in a similar way, the flash of light they see from a "shooting star" or meteor is a white-hot glow produced by the heat of friction between the meteor and the air, as the meteor falls through the Earth's atmosphere. Many smaller meteors burn up before hitting the Earth's surface—that doesn't happen on the Moon, because the Moon has no air to rub against, which is one reason why the Moon has lots of craters.

Making Craters

1. Tell the class that they will now investigate what happens when a meteoroid hits a solid surface like that of the Moon.

2. Tell the students that they will use a pan of flour and three different size rocks to investigate meteor craters. The flour will represent the surface of the Moon and the rocks will be the "meteoroids."

3. Demonstrate the technique:

> • Place an old newspaper and a pan of flour on the floor near your feet.

> • Sprinkle a light coating of instant chocolate milk mix on the surface of the flour to create a contrast that will help make changes more visible.

> • Hold out a medium-sized rock at about shoulder level. Don't actually drop the rock. Tell the students that they are to drop, **NOT THROW,** their rock onto the flour.

> • After they drop their "meteoroid" they observe what happens to the flour.

4. Ask, "What do you think will happen?" and have several students make predictions.

5. Explain that they will work in groups, and take turns dropping the rocks into the flour. Point out that they need to observe very carefully so they can describe what happens on impact and what features are created on the "lunar" surface. It's not necessary to smooth the flour and apply chocolate milk mix after each try.

6. Emphasize how important it is to drop the rocks carefully, and **never to throw the rocks,** or act in any way that is unsafe. (Since flour underfoot can be slippery, if any gets on the floor it should be swept up immediately. Demonstrate how to

sweep flour onto a sheet of newspaper and return it to the basin.)

Free Exploration

1. If you feel it would be helpful, give the students a few minutes as a whole group to discuss ways to take turns making the craters. You may also want to have them meet in their small groups to agree on a system for taking turns **before** you distribute their materials.

2. Distribute the materials to the teams and let them freely explore the materials and practice making craters for about five minutes. Do not pass out the data sheets yet.

3. After free exploration gather students away from the materials and ask the students: "What did you find out?" What features did your craters have?"

4. You may want to have a few volunteers draw what they saw on the chalkboard. As students describe the various features, write some terms on the board. [The impression left on the surface is called a *crater basin*. Students may have noticed a *rim* around the edge of the basin and streaks or *rays* that radiated outward from the crater.]

It's okay that there will be chocolate milk powder mixed in the flour as teams repeatedly level and resurface the flour. If the mixture becomes very dark, or if a team has used up all its chocolate milk powder, suggest that they sprinkle flour on the surface instead of the powder to create a contrast.

Meteor Experiments

1. Explain the procedures for the two experiments, as follows:

2. Remind your students that they saw craters of many different **sizes** on the slide of the Moon. Ask, "What might affect how **big** craters will be?" [Students may suggest meteoroid size or weight, speed at impact, direction, or type of surface material.]

3. Explain to the class that the teams will now conduct experiments to find out how two of those factors affect the size of the craters: the **size of the meteoroid** and the **speed of impact.** Hold up a data sheet and explain the two experiments:

Experiment #1: Size of Rock

• Tell the class that in order to learn more about how the size of the rock affects the size of the crater, teams will make three craters with each of their three rocks (a total of nine craters for Experiment #1). Teams will drop three different size rocks from the same height. They are to

drop each rock three times, and record the crater diameter after each drop.

• Ask why it will be important to drop all the rocks from the same height. [Then, if the crater size varies, they'll know it's because of the size of the rock.] Suggest that they use one team member's shoulder height as a standard for every trial.

• Demonstrate how to remove the rock from the flour very carefully, so you don't disturb the crater.

• Show how to measure the diameter of the crater, using a paper centimeter ruler. Show where to record the crater diameters on the data sheet.

• Demonstrate how to jiggle the container back and forth a few times to level the flour, and how to sprinkle more chocolate milk powder on top when the surface needs it.

You may want to have the students calculate averages, although the results may be evident without it.

Experiment #2: Speed of Impact

• Explain that this time, the team will choose only one rock to make all their craters, but they will drop the rock from different heights: knee-high, shoulder-high, and as high as they can reach when standing on the floor. Make sure that the students understand that a rock gains speed as it falls, so the farther it falls, the faster it will be going when it hits the flour. They will make three craters from each of the three heights. (A total of nine craters for Experiment #2.)

• Ask why they should use the same rock when they are experimenting with different speeds of "meteors." [If they used different rocks *and* different heights, they won't know which made the differences in crater sizes.]

• Point out that knee-high, shoulder-high, and as high as they can reach, may vary for different students, and ask them for ideas about how to keep the height standard on all three tries. [They could take turns dropping the rock, but use one student's knee, shoulder, and outstretched arm as the standard for all tries.]

• Show where to record all crater diameters in this second experiment.

Students Experiment

1. Make sure the students understand the two experiments. Hand out the data sheets and paper rulers and have them begin.

2. Circulate during the experiments, checking to be sure students are working safely and cooperatively in their teams.

3. If a team finishes early, suggest that they extend their investigations in Experiment #2 by, for example, **carefully** standing on a chair to drop the rock. (Older students may want to extend their investigation by observing or measuring crater *depths* created by various sizes or speeds of "meteoroids." The long "rays" that radiate from their "craters" could also be measured.)

4. As teams finish, have them return their equipment to the materials area and clean up. Students should keep their data sheets for the discussion.

Discussing the Results

1. Gather the class in the discussion area.

2. Have the class look at their data for Experiment #1, comparing meteor sizes, and ask them to describe what they observed and recorded. Ask, "Does the size of the meteoroid have anything to do with the size of the crater?" [Your students' experimental data is likely to vary, but many students will find that crater size increases with the size of the meteoroid.]

3. Ask the students what they can conclude from Experiment #2, about meteors that have struck with different speeds. [Again, student data will vary, but many students will conclude that the faster the meteor, the bigger the crater.] You may want to add that scientists estimate that real craters caused by actual meteor impacts are about 20 times the diameter of the meteor itself.

4. Show the slide of Earth's Moon again. Ask volunteers to point out some of the features of craters on the Moon that they recognize from their experiments.

5. Show the close-up of a Moon crater (Slide #13) and ask for more observations and comments. Your students may notice that all the lunar craters appear round. No matter the initial shape of the meteor (or the angle of its impact) the resulting explosion will always form a round crater.

The "Background for Teachers" contains additional information on past and present experiments and theories about craters.

Students may notice the central peaks in some craters. Modern scientists have been able to simulate actual meteor impacts with rocks fired from powerful guns (at 30,000 mph). At such speeds the meteor does not stop moving at the moment of impact. Friction rapidly heats the meteor and a tremendous explosion occurs. (Imagine quickly trying to change all the energy of a room-sized meteor traveling at 30,000 mph into heat!) If the meteor is large and fast enough, the ground liquefies, forming a crater with a rim around it. In large impacts the rim collapses, and the liquefied material rushing back into the center of the crater forms a mountain in the middle. Debris thrown out by the explosion forms rays that may extend for hundreds of miles. On Earth, small pieces of a meteor are sometimes found at the impact crater, confirming that the crater was caused by a meteor impact.

Slide 13 – "Crater close up, Earth's Moon"

Going Further

1. Craters in Liquids

For each group of four to six students, you'll need a cup of water, a medicine dropper (optional), and 1 blank sheet of paper. Begin by showing the slide of the close-up of a Moon crater again, and point out the central peak.

Explain to the students that they will experiment to see what happens when a meteor falls into a liquid, and that one of the features they should look for is the central peak. Demonstrate as follows: Pour a cup of water into a pie pan. If you are using medicine droppers, show how to hold the dropper about a foot over the pan and allow a drop of water to fall into the pan. Or, demonstrate how to dip a finger into the water so that a drop hangs from it, and shake the drop loose so it falls into the water. (Although the drop of water is a little bigger with the dropper, the fingertip method works fine.)

Encourage all members of the team to observe what happens from the side and from just above the surface of the water. Have the students take turns releasing drops and observing what happens. Each team should discuss their results and draw what they see on their papers. The students might identify the following:

> — As soon as the drop hits, it goes below the surface of the water, making sort of a "crater."

> — Ripples come from the center, hit the walls of the pan, and bounce back and forth.

> — A mound of water forms in the center of the crater, right after the drop is dropped. It may *seem* as if the drop "bounces" back after it hits the water.

Ask the students what crater features they saw that they may not have seen in the experiment with solids. [*concentric circles, ripples, and central peaks.*] Explain that very large meteors that have struck the Moon move so fast that they melt the rocks. In these cases, even though the surface may have been solid before the impact of the meteor, we can sometimes see the central peak caused when the Moon's surface turned to molten rock for a few minutes, then solidified before the peak had a chance to become level again.

2. Moon Mapping

If you wanted to land a spacecraft or build a lunar settlement on the Moon, where would you choose? Before real astronauts landed on the Moon, they needed to study a map of the Moon. Hand out a copy of the Moon Map (page 29) to each student. Project the slide image of the full moon (slide #12) and have students compare the features on their map with those on the Moon's surface.

Have the students work in pairs or groups and assign a particular "ocean," "sea," or "bay" for them to find. They should locate it first on their map and then identify the corresponding feature on the slide. Those who finish quickly can practice finding other features. Have volunteers from each group get up and point out their feature to the rest of the class. (There are 12 oceans and seas labeled on the map.)

For a more difficult challenge, assign each group a crater or mountain range to find. Invite the students to use their lunar maps when observing the real Moon in the sky. Encourage them to use a pair of binoculars if available. (Through binoculars, the moon-view will match the map, but through a telescope, the image is reversed!)

3. Rabbit in the Moon

Show the moon slide again. Ask the students if they can see a rabbit. Ask where are the ears? Where is the tail? Tell the class that many Native American cultures associated the moon with a rabbit. Duplicate the rabbit pictures on page 100 for each student. Tell them that the rabbit is a depiction of the rabbit in the moon found on pottery of the Mimbres tribe, who lived in what is now the Southwestern United States from the 9th to 12th centuries. (One piece of Mimbres pottery, which shows a burst of light below the leg of a rabbit, is believed to depict the supernova that created the Crab nebula in 1054!) The Japanese and many other cultures around the world also visualize a "rabbit in the moon." Suggest that next time your students look at the real moon in the sky, they look for the rabbit—it's easy to see!

Name _____   Date _____

CRATERS

Experiment 1: Size of Meteoroid
How will the size of the rock affect the size of the crater?

Record the Crater Diameter for:

	1st try	2nd try	3rd try
Small rock	_____	_____	_____
Medium rock	_____	_____	_____
Large rock	_____	_____	_____

What can you conclude?
_____
_____
_____

Experiment 2: Speed of Meteoroid
How will the speed of impact affect the size of the crater?

Record the Crater Diameter for:

	1st try	2nd try	3rd try
Slow	_____	_____	_____
Medium	_____	_____	_____
Fast	_____	_____	_____

What can you conclude?
_____
_____
_____

MM   1 2 3 4 5 6 7 8 9 10 11 12 13 14 15

MOON MAP

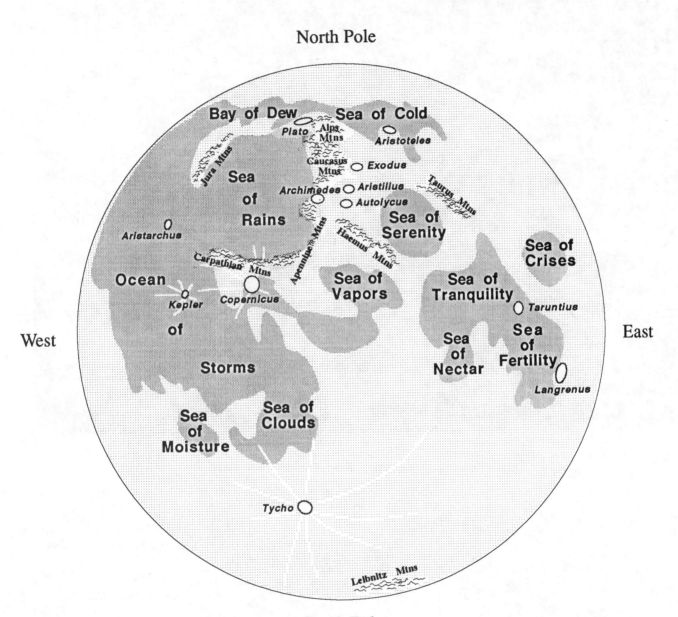

North Pole

West   East

South Pole

LHS GEMS—*The Moons of Jupiter*

Activity 3:
A Scale Model of the Jupiter System

Overview

Your class begins this session with a scale model of the Earth-Moon system. By using the same scale to model the Jupiter system, your students gain an understanding of the large sizes of the moons of Jupiter, and the enormous distances that separate them. While they may be surprised at the distance from Earth to its Moon, your students will be astonished by the scale of the Jupiter system. Because the Jupiter system will not fit in the classroom at this scale, you are asked to bring your students outside for the second half of this session. However, if going outside isn't possible, you can still communicate the vastness of the system by modeling just Jupiter and its innermost large moon in the classroom.

Because the concept of scale explored in this session may be difficult for younger students, fourth grade teachers may wish to skip this session and go on to Session 4.

What You Need

For the class:
- ❑ 1 meter stick
- ❑ 1 roll of tape (masking or clear)
- ❑ an Earth globe (or blue balloon, or ball) about 25 cm, or 10 inches in diameter
- ❑ 2 white balloons or balls (about 7 cm, or 3 inches in diameter, inflated)
- ❑ a model car or any other example of a *scale model*
- ❑ a piece of chalk
- ❑ a pair of scissors
- ❑ a length of string 1.5 meters (5 feet) long
- ❑ a thick black felt pen and assorted crayons
- ❑ 4 manila file folders
- ❑ 1 copy of the data sheets for Session 4 (master on pages 49, 50), used as described in Getting Ready for the Jupiter Scale Model, #5, below.

Getting Ready

For the Earth-Moon Scale Model:

1. Blow up a blue balloon to 25 cm (10") in diameter (or have handy an Earth globe or a ball that size). You will also need two white balloons or balls about 7 cm, or 3" in diameter. Keep the Earth balloon and *one* of the moon balloons near the place where you will introduce the session. The moon balloon should be out of sight of the students as you begin your introduction.

2. Measure a distance of 7.7 meters (about 25 feet) from the Earth balloon to a side or back wall. Tape the other moon balloon on the wall at that spot, high enough to be seen when you are ready to point it out to the class. If you are using a ball that can't be taped to the wall, place it on a shelf or other surface.

For the Jupiter System Scale Model:

1. During the activity, you will need to draw a big circle or arc on the chalkboard to represent Jupiter. To make a circle the right size, tie one end of the length of string to a piece of chalk. Use a meter stick to measure the string, starting from the chalk, to 1.43 meters (about 4 feet, 8 inches). Cut the string at that point.

2. Practice using the chalk and string to draw an arc on the chalkboard. Although you will probably not be able to fit the complete circle on the chalkboard, adjust the string so that you are able to draw as much of a circle as possible. Erase the arc, and have the chalk and string ready so that you can draw it again during the activity.

3. Read through the session and decide whether it will be possible to bring your class outside to pace off the distances from Jupiter to its four biggest moons. (**This requires a distance of at least 38 meters, or about 124 feet.**)

If it is *not* possible to go outside:

> • Plan to end the session after Jupiter Scale Model, #4, page 35, below. In the classroom, you'll model the chalkboard Jupiter and only its first moon, and compare them to the Earth-Moon model.

> • You may still want to give your students a sense of the vast distances to the other three moons by simply telling

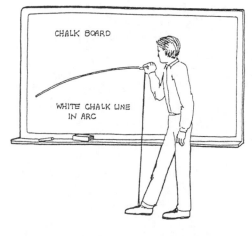

Another way to make a big Jupiter on the wall is to use an overhead projector and transparency to project a circle 2.9 meters in diameter (a bit over 9 feet). Move the projector back or forward until the circle is the right size.

them where in the school the other moons would be at this scale. Prepare by using the chart on page 35 to pace off distances in the building from your chalkboard Jupiter to the other three moons. **You can approximate a meter with a long stride.** Then in class, you'll be able to amaze your students by saying, for instance, that Callisto would be 38 meters away—in the cafeteria!

See the "Going Further" ideas for this activity on page 37 for a other ways to model the scale of the Jupiter system without leaving the classroom.

4. If you *can* go outside, choose an area on the school grounds where your class will have a 38-meter (124 feet) clear line of sight, preferably with a wall at one end. Using your chalk and string again, draw another chalk circle representing Jupiter on the wall. If this is not possible, look for some object outdoors that is about 3 meters (9 feet) in diameter that can be used to represent Jupiter.

5. Prepare four manila folders as follows to show the sizes of the moons in the scale model, and to use as markers in the outdoor scale model. First, make one copy of each of the two "Grand Tour" data sheets from Session 4 (pages 49 and 50). Outline the four moons with a thick black marker, color them with crayon, and cut them out. Tape each one onto a different manila folder. With the felt pen, write the name of each moon on its folder in large letters so that it can be read when the folder is held as shown at right.

GO!

Introducing Scale Models

1. Begin by asking the students to give examples of scale models. [Students may suggest maps, pictures, a globe of the Earth, toy cars or airplanes, etc.]

2. Explain that some toy cars may look exactly like the real thing because everything is "to scale." (Hold up a model car if you have one. If not draw a simple model car on the chalkboard.) Someone measured all the parts of a real car and made each part smaller by exactly the same amount. Maybe 1 meter on the real car equals 1 centimeter on the model. Point out that on a map or a globe of the Earth, many miles may equal one inch. When you look at a map or globe, it looks like the real thing, only smaller.

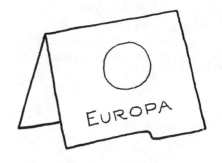

3. Tell the students that they'll work together as a whole class in this session. First, they will get a better idea of the sizes in the Earth-Moon system by using a scale model. Then they will compare the Earth-Moon system to the Jupiter System, using the same scale.

Presenting the Earth-Moon Scale Model

1. Hold up the blue balloon (or globe or ball), and tell the students that it represents the planet Earth. Every centimeter on the balloon represents 500 km on the real Earth. (Scale of 1 cm = 500 km.) That means that everything in our model will be *50 million times smaller* than in real life.

2. Help your students grasp the meaning of the scale by asking them to hold up their fingers and show you how big 1 cm is. Explain that in this scale model, the distance of 1 cm in the model represents 500 km, or about 311 miles in the real world. Give an example of how far that distance would be by referring to the distance from the school to a well-known place.

3. Ask, "How big do you think the Moon would be on this scale?" (Accept a few guesses.) Hold up the white balloon (or smaller ball) and let them see the comparative sizes of the Earth and Moon.

4. Make the "Moon" orbit the "Earth." Ask the class to guess how far away the Moon should be, as it orbits the Earth in this scale model. Should it be a few centimeters away? A meter?

5. After they've made a few guesses, point to the white balloon that you positioned earlier, and say that at this scale, the Moon would be 7.7 meters (about 25 feet) from the Earth! Ask them to imagine the white balloon going in a big orbit around the blue balloon, always staying the same distance away. Ask, "Will the moon's whole orbit fit in the classroom?" [No]

You may want to tell the students that if we were to add the Sun to our scale model, it would be 28 meters (91 feet) in diameter, and almost 3 kilometers (2 miles) away. If the Earth were at the center of the Sun, the entire Moon's orbit would fit inside the Sun with lots of room to spare!

The Jupiter System Scale Model

1. Ask the class, "If the Earth and Moon were the size of these balloons, how big do you think Jupiter would be?" Accept a few guesses.

2. Using the chalk and string you prepared earlier, draw an arc on the chalkboard. Tell the class that this is the size of Jupiter **at the same scale** we have been using. Ask the students to imagine that the circle is complete, and to picture it as a ball shape. Hold up the Earth balloon for comparison, and say that **if Jupiter were hollow, about 1,000 Earths could be jammed together inside. (Three Earths could fit in Jupiter's famous red spot!)**

3. Tell your students that one of the biggest problems the first explorers to Jupiter will have to overcome is understanding just how huge the Jupiter system is! Ask them if they recall which one of the four moons they tracked in Session 1 orbited closest to Jupiter. [Io] Hold up the manila folder with Io drawn to scale. Ask if they think Io is bigger or smaller than Earth's Moon. [Slightly bigger.] Hold up your manila folders with Europa, Ganymede, and Callisto for a comparison of sizes. Explain that the moons are all drawn to the same scale: 1 cm = 500 km.

4. Ask for guesses about how far Io would be from the picture of Jupiter you drew on the chalkboard. Accept all answers. Reveal that Io would be about eight meters from the chalkboard. Hold up the meter stick and say that it is about one giant step long. Ask for a volunteer to pace off eight giant steps, and have her hold the manila folder of Io there as a marker.

5. Tell the class that the next furthest large moon from Jupiter is Europa, at about 13 meters in this scale. Will this fit in the classroom? [Probably not.] Explain that, to get all four moons in the scale model, the class will need to go outside. Explain that the class will gather at the Jupiter "mark" you have prepared, and together, you will all pace out the distances to each of the four moons. Bring with you the four manila folders and the distance information below. *Distances between moons are listed here in this scale, then the table below shows the actual distances between the moons and Jupiter.*

Jupiter to Io: 8 meters
Io to Europa: 5 meters
Europa to Ganymede: 8 meters
Ganymede to Callisto: 17 meters

Name of Moon	Actual Distance from Jupiter	Distance in Scale Model	Convert to Whole Meters
Io	421,600 km	843 cm	8 meters
Europa	670,900 km	1342 cm	13 meters
Ganymede	1,070,000 km	2140 cm	21 meters
Callisto	1,883,000 km	3766 cm	38 meters

Pacing the Distances

1. Have everyone stand side by side at the place where you decided Jupiter would be. Put the meter stick on the ground and have all the students practice taking one giant step and then returning to Jupiter. Then have the class pace off eight meters from Jupiter along with you. Have one student hold the scale drawing of Io on the folder at about the distance where most of the class ended up after eight paces.

2. Have the class look back toward Jupiter. Ask them to imagine that Io makes a huge orbit around Jupiter. How long does it take for the real Io to go around Jupiter? [about 2 days.] Tell the class that Jupiter has 16 known moons, and that four of the small moons are orbiting between Io and the planet. (If it is difficult to be heard by the whole class while outdoors, you may want to save additional information about the moons for your concluding discussion indoors.)

3. Have the student marking Io's orbit stay in place, holding the folder. With the rest of the class, continue to pace off the other three moons, leaving a student holding a folder at each.

4. When they reach the last moon, Callisto, ask the students to turn and face away from Jupiter. Tell them that eight of Jupiter's small moons are even **farther away** from the planet than Callisto. The farthest one, Sinope, would be about half a kilometer (or a quarter of a mile) away at this scale.

5. Have everyone turn and look back at the Galilean moons and Jupiter. Ask them to remember the balloon model of Earth and its Moon in the classroom. Remind them that this is the same scale. The Jupiter system is MUCH BIGGER!

6. Ask the students to picture the four moons orbiting Jupiter. Would all the moons be lined up the way they are now in your model? [No. Since they move at different speeds and in different orbits, they would usually be at different parts of their orbits at any one time.]

7. If there's time, bring the students back to Jupiter, leaving the manila folders in place to mark the positions of the Galilean moons. Ask them to look out and see how large the moons appear from the viewpoint of an explorer near Jupiter's surface.

8. After returning to the classroom, explain that the planets of the Solar System revolve around the Sun in the same way as the moons orbit Jupiter. And though the Jupiter system is huge, the Solar System is much, much bigger. You may want

One teacher modified the activity so that his students formed a chain, touching outstretched arms to mark the distances to the moons. Each student's armspan was about a meter, so eight students with outstretched arms in a line reach from Jupiter to Io. (Since it's 38 meters to Callisto, he must have "borrowed" a few extra students!)

1993: Jan. 14 a

to tell them that at this scale, the Sun would be 27.7 meters (91 feet) in diameter. Ask for guesses about how far away from Jupiter the Sun would be at this scale. [Jupiter's orbit would be 15 kilometers (10 miles) from the Sun!]

Back in the classroom, you may want to provide your students with more information about Jupiter and its 16 moons, as well as other planets, the Sun, and the nearest star. Further information on the 16 moons is provided in "Background for Teachers" and "Recommended Reading" at the end of the book.

Going Further

1. Calculations for the Model of Jupiter and its Moons

You can challenge your students to check the calculations for the scale model of Jupiter given in the activity to see if they are accurate. Here's how to do it.

a. Recall that the scale of the model is 1 cm = 500 km.

b. The *scale factor*, which has the value of 1, is: $\frac{1\ cm}{500\ km}$

c. To find the radius (R) and distance (D) of each of the moons in the model, multiply it by the scale factor. For Ganymede:

$$R\ (Ganymede) = \frac{1\ cm}{500\ km} \times 2,600\ km = 5.2\ cm$$

$$D\ (Ganymede) = \frac{1\ cm}{500\ km} \times 1,070,000\ km = 2,140\ cm = 21.4\ meters$$

d. Have your students use calculators to complete the table, using the scale factor: $\frac{1\ cm}{500\ km}$

	Real Radius	Model Radius	Real Distance	Model Distance
Jupiter	71,600 km		0 km	
Io	1,800 km		421,600 km	
Europa	1,600 km		670,900 km	
Ganymede	2,600 km	5.2 cm	1,070,000 km	21.4 meters
Callisto	2,400 km		1,883,000 km	

Teacher's Answer Key:

	Real Radius	Model Radius	Real Distance	Model Distance
Jupiter	71,600 km	1.43 meters	0 km	0 meters
Io	1,800 km	3.6 cm	421,600 km	8.4 meters
Europa	1,600 km	3.2 cm	670,900 km	13.4 meters
Ganymede	2,600 km	5.2 cm	1,070,000 km	21.4 meters
Callisto	2,400 km	4.8 cm	1,883,000 km	37.7 meters

2. Making a Smaller Scale Model of the Jupiter System

It is possible to set up a smaller scale model of Jupiter and all four of its large moons in the classroom rather than outside. This has the advantage of convenience (especially for days of cold or stormy weather). However, it adds some confusion because it is a different scale from the one that is used for the scale models used in both Session 3 and 4. Therefore, this "Going Further" activity is recommended only for students who are very comfortable with the concept of scale.

Start by doing Session 3 as described in the main text of this guide, up to and including the classroom model of Jupiter and Io, and pointing out how far it would be to the other moons in Jupiter's system. Ask the students: "How can we make a model of Jupiter and its moons that will fit inside the classroom?" [Change the scale!] Suggest that they use a scale *ten times smaller*, where 1 cm = 5,000 km. At that scale the Earth would be about 2.5 cm, or about 1 inch in diameter. Ask, "How big would Earth's Moon be at this scale?" [about the size of a marble.]

As described in the previous "Going Further" activity, have your students use calculators to complete the table, using the scale factor: 1 cm
                  5,000 km

	Real Radius	Model Radius	Real Distance	Model Distance
Jupiter	71,600 km		0 km	
Io	1,800 km		421,600 km	
Europa	1,600 km		670,900 km	
Ganymede	2,600 km	5.2 cm	1,070,000 km	2.14 meters
Callisto	2,400 km		1,883,000 km	

If your students have done the previous "Going Further" activity, they will see that they do not need their calculators for this one! They just make all of the model distances and sizes smaller by a factor of ten by moving the decimal point one place to the left.

At this scale, students can now make paper models of the Jupiter system using an open file folder for Jupiter, and small bits of clay for its moons. The students should use a meter stick to measure distances, and can record their measurements on a strip of adding machine tape. They can be assigned to work in small groups to create their models, or work individually to make models to take home and decorate their rooms.

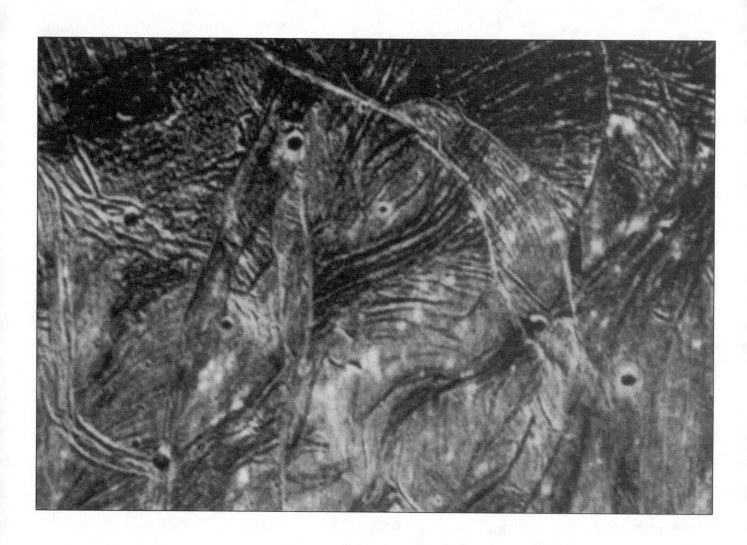

Activity 4:
"Grand Tour" of the Jupiter System

Overview

In this activity, your students continue their exploration of the Jupiter system by studying close-up views of Jupiter's four major moons that were taken by the Voyager spacecraft. These beautiful glimpses of distant moons will inspire wonder and imagination in your students, just as they did in the scientists who first saw them. The "Grand Tour" will also allow your students to practice the skills of observation, recording data, critical discussion, and making careful inferences based on evidence.

Students will discover some major features of the moons, and see how they are similar and different. They'll draw the moon features on data sheets, using the same scale used in the previous session. Since the "Grand Tour" often prompts enthusiastic discussion, you may wish to allow more than one class session for this activity.

What You Need

For the Class:
❑ 1 slide projector
❑ The Teacher Fact Sheets, pages 45–48
❑ Slide Set, including:

>   # 14 Jupiter, with two moons
>   # 15 Close-up of the Red Spot
>   # 16 Callisto
>   # 17 Callisto Close-up
>   # 18 Ganymede
>   # 19 Ganymede Close-up
>   # 20 Europa
>   # 21 Europa Close-up
>   # 22 Io
>   # 23 Io Close-up

For each team of 4–5 students:
❑ 1 box of crayons

For each student:
❑ 1 pencil
❑ data sheets (masters on pages 49, 50)

>   Callisto and Ganymede
>   Io and Europa with the US map for scale

Getting Ready

1. Copy the two data sheets for each student.

2. Set up the slide projector with slides 14–23, and look at them yourself. Since students will need enough light to draw during the slide activity, decide how to partially darken the room.

3. Read the Teacher Fact Sheets. You will probably also want to read over the information about Jupiter's moons in the "Background for Teachers" section.

Jupiter's Four Largest Moons

1. Tell the class that they will now go on an imaginary journey to the Jupiter system to "visit" each of the four Galilean moons. Although no one from Earth has ever visited Jupiter, we do have pictures of Jupiter and its moons that were taken by two Voyager spacecraft. Voyager radioed these pictures back to Earth, where computers translated the radio signal into the pictures the class is about to see. These images and others like them are still being studied by scientists.

2. Hand out the data sheets, and tell the class that the moons drawn on them are in the same scale as the Jupiter system scale model in the last session (1 cm = 500 km) and that the map of the United States is there to help give them an idea of the sizes. Ask which moon is the biggest [Ganymede] and which the smallest [Europa, which is about the size of Earth's Moon]. Tell them they will begin with the data sheet for Callisto and Ganymede. Organize the students into teams so they can share crayons.

3. Dim the lights, but have the room light enough so students can write and draw. Announce that the "Grand Tour" is about to begin, and that it will start with a fly-by of Jupiter itself! (They won't need their data sheets until they tour the moons.) As you show the two slides of Jupiter, (#14 and #15) ask the students for their observations and ideas. (Slide #15 is a **composite image** of Earth and Jupiter's red spot.) Spend a short time sharing with them some of the information about Jupiter from the "Background for Teachers" section. Be sure to include:

> • The beautiful stripes are bands of clouds. Jupiter probably does not have a solid surface. If you tried to land on the planet, your spacecraft would sink through clouds until the pressure was so great that the craft would be crushed.

Slide #14 is one of the most striking images from Voyager 1. Two moons, Io and Europa, appear against the vast planetary backdrop. (Io is above the Red Spot.) By looking at the moons can you say where the Sun must have been when this picture was taken?

• The Great Red Spot is thought to be a giant storm that has been in existence for at least 300 years. In it can be seen deeper layers of Jupiter's atmosphere.

• Jupiter spins, or rotates on its axis, very rapidly—once every 10 hours. (Earth takes 24 hours.)

4. Explain that the tour will now go to the outermost large moon, Callisto, and then travel inward to the other three moons. **For each moon**, guide the "Grand Tour" as follows:

• Start with open-ended questions that encourage creative and imaginative observations, such as "What do you see?" and "What does it look like to you?" Show both slides for each moon. (There are two slides for each moon, showing two views, wide-angle and close-up.)

• Have the students write, on the back of their data sheets, five words that come to mind as they look at the colors and shapes in the moonscape. Ask them to share some of their favorite descriptive words that come to mind. Tell them that other scientists have made fanciful observations, too. For example, it was late at night when the first images of Io were received from Voyager 1. The imaging scientists were hungry, and one commented that Io looked like a pizza!

• Guide the students in recognizing how large the moons are by comparing each of the moons with the map of the United States. For example, "If Io really were a pizza, how big would a piece of pepperoni be?" [about the size of Texas!]

• Now ask the students to study the moon again, this time as scientists making maps.

• Ask them to draw, as closely as possible, where the main features are and about how big they are, compared to the whole side of the moon. Suggest that they sketch the general size of the features lightly in pencil, before filling in details and colors. Show the slide of the view of the entire moon for a few more minutes, then the close-up. Go back to the first slide if students request it.

• Throughout the tour, help your students distinguish between **evidence** (what they observe— for example, that Europa has dark lines), and **inference** (what they conclude from the evidence—for example, that Europa's lines are cracks in an icy surface). Tell the students that their observations provide *evidence* on which to base

*The term **rotate** (or **rotation**) refers to the motion of a body spinning on its axis, as the Earth rotates once in 24 hours. **Revolve** (or **revolution**) refers to the motion of a body in orbit, as the Earth revolves around the Sun every 365-1/4 days.*

Slide 14

Slide 15

*One fourth grade teacher told us, "The students **loved** this activity. Their discussion was wonderful; I wish I had taped it. They saw faces, creatures, "things" in the moonscapes, and they had great ideas about what made the colors and shapes!"*

Some teachers and their students have noticed specks and other imperfections in the photographs. Remember that the data for the images had to travel several hundred million kilometers through space. It's really quite remarkable how good the images are! The occasional "glitch" in data is known as an "artifact" on the image.

You might tell the students that the moons of Jupiter all keep one side facing the planet as they orbit. (This is true for Earth's Moon, too.) The Voyager pictures show different sides of the moons than an imaginary inhabitant of Jupiter would see, because Voyager's path through the Jupiter system allowed many varied views of the moons.

conclusions. Ideas and conclusions that they make, based on careful study of evidence, are called *inferences*. Scientists constantly make inferences from evidence, and refine these inferences as they learn more.

• As they sketch the features, share some information about the moon from the teacher fact sheets. (The first paragraph on each teacher fact sheet includes information noted on the student sheets. After that there is further information, both for the full moon view and the close-up view.) After the students have completed each drawing, ask them to compare the sizes of the various features with the map of the United States sketched beside it. Then go on to the next moon!

5. When you have done this for all four moons, and thus finished the "Grand Tour," turn on the lights, and point out to the students that they have acted just as scientists do who study the moons of Jupiter. For example, they have observed the photographs carefully, discussed and recorded information, compared the moon features with other things we know about, and ventured some possible ideas, explanations, or tentative conclusions from what they have observed.

A wonderful accompaniment to this *Moons of Jupiter* unit, (especially relevant to the "Grand Tour") is the GEMS unit entitled *Oobleck: What Do Scientists Do?* In the *Oobleck* activities, students investigate a substance said to come from another planet. Throughout the *Oobleck* unit, students are involved in similar processes as the scientists who studied photographs taken during the Viking Mission to Mars.

Teacher Fact Sheet　　Callisto

Entire moon view:

Callisto is a world of craters. Impact craters cover much of the surface of the moon. The bright spots are probably ice exposed by the impact of large meteors. The largest crater is called Valhalla (Vahl-HAH-lah). The bright area is 300 km (186 miles) in diameter, and the largest ring around Valhalla is 3,000 km (1865 miles) in diameter. There are no tall mountains or volcanoes on Callisto.

- Callisto is about the size of the planet Mercury. Although Callisto is probably over four billion years old, most of its craters were most likely made in the first half billion years.
- The surface is very old.
- Callisto is composed of a mixture of ice and rock. The dark areas are dust and rock. Fresh meteor impact craters show a very light-colored icy layer under the darker surface rock.
- Not only are there no mountains, but even the crater rims are very low.
- The surface temperature on Callisto is between –100° C and –200° C. (–148° F and –328° F) At that frigid temperature, ice is as hard as quartz is on Earth.

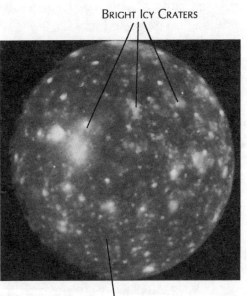

BRIGHT ICY CRATERS

DARK ROCKY SURFACE

Close-up view:

- The largest feature on Callisto is a huge ancient crater called Valhalla. It is surrounded by concentric rings of bright ridges. A crater of this sort has never been seen before on any other moon or planet.

UNSOLVED MYSTERY:

- **If Valhalla is an impact crater, why does it have a multiple ring structure unlike other craters?**

Teacher Fact Sheet   Ganymede

Entire moon view:

Ganymede is the largest moon in the entire solar system. The dark areas are the most ancient, and are similar to the surface of Callisto. (Point out the dark area called Galileo Regio. (REH-jee-oh) Also like Callisto, the bright places are probably impact craters that reveal ice under the rock. Light brown areas show long ridges of mountains and valleys

in close-up views.

- Like Callisto, Ganymede is made up of a mixture of ice and rocks.
- Let's take a close-up look at the light brown areas.

BRIGHT IMPACT CRATERS

GALILEO REGIO

Close-up view:

- All of these grooves are ridges of mountains and valleys, similar in scale to the Appalachian Mountains in the Eastern United States. These mountains may have formed like Earth's mountains, by movements of Ganymede's crust over millions of years.

UNSOLVED MYSTERY:

- **How did the grooved terrain come to be?**
  (While these mountains may have been formed like the Earth's mountains, the mechanism for this happening in an *icy crust* remains a mystery.)

Teacher Fact Sheet   E u r o p a

Entire moon view:

Europa has the smoothest surface in the solar system. There are no craters visible at all. The slightly darker region may be a little rougher than the rest of Europa's surface. The surface appears to be criss-crossed by dark lines. They may be cracks, but aren't too deep. No one knows for certain what they are.

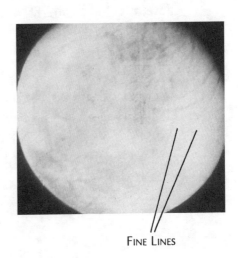

FINE LINES

- In this image, the moon is covered almost completely by a thin icy crust. There may be a 10 km deep ocean of liquid water under the ice! Possibly the smooth surface is created by a mixture of ice and water that comes up through cracks in the surface, repairing cracks with a thin layer of ice. On the other hand, some scientists suspect that Europa is covered with ice from volcanoes that erupt water.
- Some scientists suspect that the dark areas may be sulfur from the volcanoes of Io. Living on Europa might be something like living in Antarctica on Earth, except that it is much colder on Europa! (Surface temperature is below −100° C (−148° F).

Close-up view:

- The dark lines vary in width from several kilometers to about 70 kilometers (43 miles) and the longest are several thousand kilometers in length.
- The lines seem to be cracks in the surface, but they are no more than 100 meters deep, which is quite shallow, compared to their width and length. It's as if someone took a huge felt pen and marked the surface! Perhaps they are cracks that have been filled with water that quickly froze; or possibly we are seeing dark rocks under the ice. On an exact scale model of Europa the size of a ping pong ball, the lines would be no thicker than the ink line from a pen.

UNSOLVED MYSTERY:

- **Why is Europa so smooth?**

Entire moon view:

Io wins the prize for the most volcanic body in the solar system. No impact craters are visible, but 200 volcanoes were counted, nine of them erupting at the time of the Voyager fly–by! The brilliant colors of red, orange, and yellow are all colors of sulfur or sulfur compounds. (Sulfur, when heated to different temperatures, can be any of these colors.)

Point out the following three volcanoes. **Pele** (PAY-lay) is an erupting volcano. The heart-shaped marking is the cloud of material being thrown out by the volcano. **Loki Patera** (LO-kee Pah-TEH-rah) is surrounded by a dark lake of liquid sulfur. **Babbar Patera** (BAH-bahr Pah-TEH-rah) was erupting when the Voyager Spacecraft flew by.

LOKI PATERA

PELE

BABBAR PATERA

- Io is the closest of the large moons to Jupiter.
- The dark spots are the centers of volcanoes.
- The circular areas are probably lakes of liquid sulfur. What would it smell like on Io? [Rotten eggs!]

Close-up view:

- Ask the students to find the erupting volcano on the edge of the planet.
- The volcanoes on Io were more violent than any in recorded history on Earth. Sulfur was ejected from the volcanoes at speeds between 300 and 1,000 meters per second (670–2237 mph) and reached heights of between 70 and 280 kilometers (43-272 miles).
- The volcanoes are probably caused by the force of Jupiter's gravity which pulls on the near side of Io more than it pulls on the far side. This difference in gravity compresses the interior of Io, causing it to heat up, and producing the volcanoes. This effect is known as "tidal pumping." (The same effect might also cause liquid water on Europa, despite surface temperatures there well below the freezing point of matter.)
- The lakes of liquid sulfur are quite hot, over 70° C, by comparison with surrounding areas that are – 180 C (–300° F). The center of Pele is about 230° C (440° F).

UNSOLVED MYSTERY:

- **Why does Io have so much sulfur?**

Name_____ Date_____

Grand Tour

Callisto

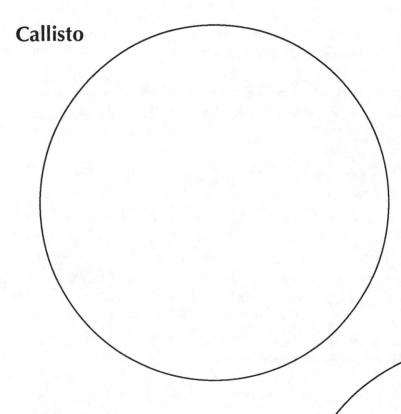

1. Impact craters cover much of the surface of Callisto.

2. The bright spots are probably ice exposed by the impact of large meteors.

3. The largest crater is called **Valhalla**. The bright area is 300 km in diameter, and the largest ring around Valhalla is 3,000 km in diameter.

4. There are no tall mountains and no volcanoes on Callisto.

Ganymede

1. **Galileo Regio** is a dark area, probably very old.

2. Bright impact craters probably reveal ice under the rock.

3. Light brown areas show long ridges of mountains and valleys in close-up views.

Note: Jupiter's moons are drawn to scale.
Scale: 1 cm = 500 km

Grand Tour

Europa

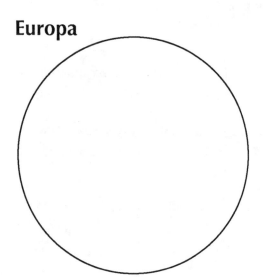

1. The slightly darker region may be a little rougher than the rest of Europa's surface.

2. Fine lines on the surface appear to be cracks, but are not very deep. No one knows for certain what they are.

Io

1. **Pele** is an erupting volcano. The heart-shaped marking is the cloud of material being thrown out by the volcano.

2. **Loki Patera** is a volcano surrounded by a dark lake of liquid sulfur. **Babbar Patera** is another volcano that was erupting when the Voyager Spacecraft flew by.

4. **A close-up view** shows a volcano erupting on the horizon. The material from the volcano is ejecting in a cloud more than 200 kilometers high.

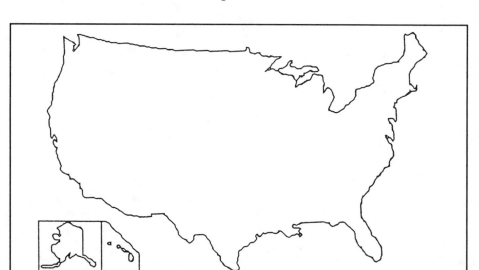

Compare the size of Jupiter's moons to the size of the United States.

All are drawn to scale.
1 cm = 500 km

"*I* was amazed at what my students were able to create and the depth of their understanding concerning the environmental problems they faced. After creating their settlements, each group presented a 'tour of the facilities' to the rest of the class. They described the function of the 'buildings' and 'machinery' they created and we displayed them."
Renee Johnson, Buffalo, New York
Grade 6.

"*T*his was a fabulous activity! I loved it and the students loved it. Some of my slower learners were able to shine. **Not one** student was incapable or unwilling. It was amazing to see."
Jane Metzger, Buffalo, New York,
Grade 4.

"*T*his activity was wonderful!! It was a great way to put the knowledge to use in a creative way! The kids had a great time and created some fantastic settlements."
Marilyn Pope, Marietta, Georgia,
Grade 8.

"*I* included a "share with the class" on an extra day where they explained functions and special circumstances related to operation. I think this made students even think more about **why** they constructed like they did. They learned **a lot** from this activity. Thanks!"
Jim Martin, Huntington Beach,
California, Grade 6.

"*M*y students could have spent days working on this. They shared their finished project with the whole group. I couldn't believe the words on their labels: "security transmitter," "receiver," "terminal," etc. Their exchanges within their groups were fun to listen to. This allowed for such creativity. It was excellent—I had a very positive classroom climate throughout! I'd give it an A!"
Cheryl Ward, Salem, Oregon,
Grade 3.

Activity 5: Creating Moon Settlements

Overview

Moons of Jupiter culminates in a creative activity in which the students work in teams to design settlements where the first explorers of the moons of Jupiter might live and work. The purposes of the activity are to review information about the moons, to imagine what it might be like to visit one of them, and to spark questions about what future explorers might learn. Student designs take unique enviromental conditions into account, thus fostering technological and creative abilities.

Most teachers allow at least two class periods for "Moon Settlements." If you have time, three periods would be even better: one to design the settlements, another to build them, and a third for teams to share their settlements with the rest of the class.

What You Need

For the class:

❏ 1 or 2 boxes of raw material or "doo-dads" for settlement building. "Doo-dad" suggestions include: plastic or paper cups, small containers (such as empty yogurt or orange juice containers), packaging material (such as plastic casings on small items, clear "bubble-wrap" and styrofoam "peanuts" and other packing materials), egg cartons, styrofoam meat trays, cardboard tubes, corks, straws, film canisters, scrap wood, colored paper or poster board, assorted stickers—YOU NAME IT!

Note: To reduce clean-up time, limit the amount of styrofoam peanuts to about four cups.

❏ 1 or 2 skeins of color yarn or string
❏ 1 or 2 rolls of foil
❏ 1 roll of plastic wrap
❏ 1 box of toothpicks
❏ 1 box of straws
❏ 1 package of blank stick-on labels (masking tape can also be used)
❏ chalk and chalkboard, or overhead projector, unused transparency, and pens
❏ Optional: tools for use by teacher or under direct supervision, such as pliers for bending wire, utility knife for cutting tubes or styrofoam, etc.

For each group of 4–5 students:
- ❑ 1 posterboard, about 30 cm x 60 cm (about 1 ft. x 2 ft.) These serve as the base for each team's settlement (size can be adjusted to your preference)
- ❑ 1 or 2 glue bottles or glue sticks
- ❑ 1 or 2 scissors
- ❑ assorted color marking pens
- ❑ 1 roll of masking or cellophane tape
- ❑ Appropriate "Scientific Mission" data sheet **for each student** (masters on pages 60-63)

Getting Ready

Before the Day of the Class:

1. Gather a few examples of the "doo-dads" listed above. Before the day of the activity, give the students a list of "doo-dads" so that they can start collecting for their projects. To give them an idea of what may be useful, show them the materials you have collected. Encourage the students to save any small objects that might turn into "space material" with a little imagination. Have them bring in their supplies from home.

2. Cut the posterboard into approximately 30 x 60 cm (1 x 2 feet) rectangles to serve as bases for each team's settlement.

3. Make enough copies of the "Scientific Missions" to Jupiter's moons (masters on pages 60-63) so that each student will have a copy of their team's mission.

The Day of the Class:

1. For quick distribution, assemble each group's supplies (glue, scissors, pens, and tape) on a tray or in a container.

2. Place the building materials in an accessible location. Students need to be able to retrieve material easily. Keep the tools such as pliers in a place that you can monitor. You could also wear a "tool belt" or carry a toolbox so you can go from group to group with all the special tools needed to assist students.

3. Arrange desks or tables and chairs so groups of 4–5 students can work together building a settlement for one of Jupiter's moons.

Many teachers gather all the "doo-dads" in one place, show the students these boxes/piles of materials, and invite teams to help themselves. Other teachers give a set of diverse materials to each team, and suggest that they trade with other teams if they need more of certain kinds of materials.

1993: Jan. 18 b

Planning Settlements on Jupiter's Moons

1. Ask the students to imagine that they are to be among the first few explorers to travel to Jupiter's moons. You may want to humorously ask them if they think they would be able to commute back and forth from Earth for their exploring work. [No way! It's too far to Jupiter to travel back and forth quickly.]

2. Tell the students that, in fact, it would take a spacecraft about **two or three YEARS** to transport people to or from the Jupiter system. How about building a settlement on Jupiter? [Not possible, as Jupiter probably has no surface. Explorers would be crushed if they tried to land. See also bottom of page 42.] Therefore, they will need to establish settlements on the moons so people can live there for long periods of time. Today, they will be working in teams to design and build a model of a settlement on one of Jupiter's moons in order to carry out a scientific mission.

3. In preparation for this mission, they first need to think about what conditions they will face. Ask them to imagine being on one of Jupiter's moons. How would things be different there? Take several answers and encourage the students to keep in mind such things as:

- Low gravity ($\frac{1}{3}$ rd to $\frac{1}{6}$ th the gravity of Earth)
- Bitter cold temperatures: –100 °C to –200°C (–148°F to –328°F) except on parts of Io
- No liquid water (except maybe on Europa)
- No air
- Little sunlight ($\frac{1}{25}$ th as much as on Earth)

- Exposure to cosmic rays and radiation. (There is intense radiation on Io, Europa, and Ganymede, because of the interactions of Jupiter's gargantuan magnetic field with the solar wind. Only Callisto lies outside Jupiter's "magnetosphere" and so has less radiation.)

4. Ask your students to think of essential items they would need to have with them or build on a moon settlement. Have the class brainstorm and list their ideas on the chalkboard or use an overhead projector.

5. Divide the class into teams of 4–5 students who work well together. Arrange seating so they can share materials and work together on the model.

6. Assign a moon to each team. Alternately you can have teams select the moon they wish, as long as each moon has at least one team assigned to settle it. If necessary, make moon assignments yourself, and assure the students that all of the moon settlements will be interesting.

Among items that have been considered essential in actual planning of similar projects are such things as: living quarters, a greenhouse, solar panels/ generators, storage facilities, a launch and landing pad, etc.

7. Explain that each moon settlement will have a different special mission. For instance, one team needs to build a hospital on its moon, to serve the needs of all four moons. Each moon also has its own special scientific goal. On Europa, for example, the mission is to use an all-terrain vehicle to explore the dark lines and determine their cause. Give each student in the group a copy of their group's "Scientific Mission" statement. Ask the students to have one member read the mission statement out loud to their group.

Building the Settlement

1. Once the teams have read their "Scientific Missions," get their attention again. Show the class a sample posterboard section and explain that they will be building their model, using a board like this as a base. Show the various raw materials they can use. If certain items are in short supply, you may want to set limits. (e.g., "Only one plastic tube per group, please!") Suggest ways for teams to be reasonable and cooperative in gathering and sharing materials.

2. Tell the students that after they have been working for a while, they will be given labels and asked to identify and label all the parts and structures they've developed. Point out the list on the chalkboard that the students brainstormed earlier; their settlement should have these essential requirements.

3. Distribute group supplies and give a posterboard to each group. Let the teams get the "raw materials," and begin planning and building. Circulate and help as needed. Ask questions and encourage the students to use their imaginations. Remind groups to keep in mind what's special about their moon, and to take those aspects into account.

4. When the settlements are well underway, bring around blank labels and have the students label each part of their settlement (launch pad, greenhouse, and so on).

5. Leave enough time at the end of class for clean up. If the students have not completed their models and you are planning more class time for them to work, encourage them to collect additional materials at home. Have them bring in these materials to incorporate into their settlements.

1993: Jan. 19 a

Discussing Lunar Settlements

1. Reporting on their projects can be a highlight of the Moons of Jupiter unit. The students have put a lot of creative energy into their model settlements, and look forward to displaying and explaining their inventions and ingenuity.

One teacher had teams imagine that they were conducting tours for visiting dignitaries!

2. Plan sufficient time for students to report. They could present a "tour of the facilities." The presentations could all be made during one class period, or spread out over two or three days.

3. Allow a few minutes for the other students to ask questions of each team. You may want to help guide and focus some discussion, with questions, such as:

- What's special about this moon?

- What were the two special objectives you had?

- How does your settlement take into account what you know about this moon?

- What do you think it would it be like to live in this settlement?

- What would you do for fun in your settlement?

- What do you think the food would be like?

- Would you really want to go on a mission like this?

4. You may want to save the structures for display at a Parent's Night or other school event. You could also have other classes visit your classroom to see the displays and hear student reports on what they learned in the unit.

5. Consider presenting or assigning one or more of the "Going Further" activities on page 59, and using this to assess growth in student knowledge. Other GEMS units, such as *Oobleck: What Do Scientists Do?* and *Earth, Moon, and Stars*, if you have not presented them already, make strong connections to this unit.

6. Students could also read and tell about a science fiction or other literature connection, or they could create their own exciting stories set on one or more of the fascinating moons of Jupiter.

• NASA TEACHER RESOURCE CENTERS •

If you live in one of these states:			Your Teacher Resource Center is:
Alaska Arizona California Hawaii	Idaho Montana Nevada Oregon	Utah Washington Wyoming	NASA Ames Research Center Teacher Resource Center Mail Stop T025 Moffett Field, CA 94035 Phone: (415) 694-3574
Connecticut Delaware D.C. Maine	Maryland Massachusetts New Hampshire New Jersey	New York Pennsylvania Rhode Island Vermont	NASA Goddard Space Flight Center Teacher Resource Laboratory Mail Code 130.3 Greenbelt, MD 20771 Phone: (301) 286-8570
Colorado Kansas Nebraska New Mexico	North Dakota Oklahoma	South Dakota Texas	NASA Johnson Space Center Teacher Resource Room Mail Code AP-4 Houston, TX 77058 Phone: (713) 483-8696
Florida Georgia Puerto Rico Virgin Islands			NASA John F. Kennedy Space Center Educators Resource Laboratory Mail Code ERL Kennedy Space Center, FL 32899 Phone: (407) 867-4090
Kentucky North Carolina South Carolina Virginia West Virginia			NASA Langley Research Center Teacher Resource Center Mail Stop 146 Hampton, VA 23665-5225 Phone: (804) 864-3293
Illinois Indiana Michigan	Minnesota Ohio Wisconsin		NASA Lewis Research Center Teacher Resource Center Mail Stop 8-1 Cleveland, OH 44135 Phone: (433-2016
Alabama Arkansas Iowa	Louisiana Missouri Tennessee		Alabama Space and Rocket Center NASA Teacher Resource Center Huntsville, AL 35807 Phone: (205) 544-5812
Mississippi			NASA Stennis Space Center Teacher Resource Center Building 1200 Stennis Space Center, MS 39520 Phone: (601) 688-3338

Going Further

1. Have the students write a story about daily life in their settlement. They may want to write a special report on an exploration to some of the unusual features of their world, or describe some of their experiments. Or, they may want to write a "letter home," describing, for example, what it is like to look up in the sky and see Jupiter instead of Earth's Moon.

2. Ask students to respond to the concern, raised by some commentators, that perhaps people should not establish settlements on other worlds. Some might say, for example, that these worlds should be left alone, so as not to be polluted or changed by human exploitation of natural resources, or by competition by governments and businesses to control specific areas or establish settlements. Do your students agree or disagree? How would they feel if missions were limited to exploration? How about setting up mines and factories on other worlds?

3. There are many great stories related to space settlement. Please refer to the Literature Connections section, Page 78.

4. Several videos about the Voyager missions are available from NASA. Videos can be ordered from your nearest local NASA Teacher Resource Center. The Jet Propulsion Laboratory Teacher Resource Center specializes in inquiries related to space and planetary exploration, and other JPL activities. That address is listed below. Other NASA Centers are listed on the previous page.

> Jet Propulsion Laboratory
> Teacher Resource Center
> JPL Educational Outreach
> Mail Stop CS-530
> Pasadena, CA 91109
> Phone: (818) 354-6916

Scientific Mission to Io

Background:

Io is one of the strangest bodies in the solar system. Its volcanoes erupt various compounds of sulfur that have the striking colors of: red, orange, yellow, black, and white. There are about 200 volcanic craters with diameters greater than 20 kilometers. Nine eruptions were recorded by the two Voyager fly-by missions in 1979. Some of the plumes were hundreds of kilometers high. The sulfurous lava flows are hundreds of kilometers long.

There are two theories about why Io has so many volcanoes. One is that it is pushed and pulled by Jupiter's strong gravity, causing it to heat up as it orbits. (This is like the way a paper clip heats up when you bend it back and forth many times.) The other suggests that the heating is caused by Jupiter's strong magnetic field.

Your Scientific Objective: Use an all-terrain electric vehicle to explore volcanoes. Be careful! They are thought to be very hot and may erupt unpredictably.

Your Permanent Settlement Objective: Import water from Europa. Develop a system for using heat energy from the volcanoes to turn the ice into water for drinking, oxygen for breathing, and hydrogen for fuel.

Don't forget about conditions like:

- Low gravity (1/3rd to 1/6th the gravity of Earth)
- Bitter cold temperatures (-100°C to -200°C), except in lava lake and volcanoes, where temperatures can be well over 70°C (160°F)
- Exposure to cosmic rays and radiation
- No liquid water
- No air
- Little sunlight (1/25th as much as on Earth)

Good Luck!

1993: Jan. 20 a

Scientific Mission to Europa

Background:

Europa is the most mysterious of Jupiter's satellites. Its surface is one of the smoothest in the solar system. There are no craters larger than 50 kilometers across. This means that Europa may undergo some sort of resurfacing process that may still be occurring. Europa's rocky interior is covered by an icy crust not more than 100 kilometers thick, but possibly as thin as a few hundred meters. There may be an ocean or layer of liquid water, extending as deep as 10 kilometers below the ice. No one knows for certain what the long dark lines are. The large dark areas may be places where Europa has been bombarded by sulfurous material originating from Io.

Your Scientific Objective:
Use an all-terrain electric vehicle to explore the dark lines and try to determine their cause. Also drill to determine the depth of ocean and the thickness of surface ice.

Your Permanent Settlement Objective:
Establish a system to mine surface ice for export to Io where it will be melted and turned into drinking water, oxygen for breathing, and hydrogen for energy.

Don't forget about conditions like:

- Low gravity (1/3rd to 1/6th the gravity of Earth)
- Bitter cold temperatures (-100°C to -200°C)
- Exposure to cosmic rays and radiation
- There may be a layer of liquid water below the ice
- No air
- Little sunlight (1/25th as much as on Earth)

Good Luck!

Scientific Mission to Ganymede

Background:

Ganymede is the largest moon in the solar system. The light regions have parallel sets of ridges. They are low mountains, somewhat like the Appalachians on Earth. The dark areas resemble the heavily cratered surface of Callisto and are believed to be older than the light areas.

Your Scientific Objective: Use an all-terrain vehicle to make a survey of the light areas and dark areas to try to determine their origins.

Your Permanent Settlement Objective: Construct a hospital to serve all four moon settlements.

Don't forget about conditions like:

- Low gravity (1/3rd to 1/6th the gravity of Earth)
- Bitter cold temperatures (-100°C to -200°C)
- Exposure to cosmic rays and radiation
- No liquid water
- No air
- Little sunlight (1/25th as much as on Earth)

Good Luck!

© 1993: Jan. 20 b

Scientific Mission to Callisto

Background:

Callisto has an ice crust of unknown depth. Callisto is almost completely covered with large craters. Most of the craters are believed to be very old — close to 4 billion years. The craters are much flatter than craters formed on rocky moons like Earth's Luna. It is not known whether the flatness of the craters on Callisto is caused by melting of the surface when a meteor strikes, or by the very slow movement of the ice over millions of years.

Your Scientific Objective: Use an all-terrain electric vehicle to make a detailed map of the rings surrounding Valhalla.

Your Permanent Settlement Objective: Make a food production facility that can supply food for all the settlements (less radiation shielding to protect farms would be required on Callisto).

Don't forget about conditions like:

- Low gravity (1/3rd to 1/6th the gravity of Earth)
- Bitter cold temperatures (-100°C to -200°C)
- Exposure to cosmic rays and radiation (though less radiation than on the other moons)
- No liquid water
- No air
- Little sunlight (1/25th as much as on Earth)

Good Luck!

Jupiter's 4 Largest Moons

Ganymede's the largest moon
Which through our system moves
Ridged mountain peaks and valleys
Make "ganymedan" grooves.

Callisto is a cratered world
(That much we've figured out)
Valhalla of the many rings
How did that come about?

Europa's surface smooth as silk
No craters do we see
Yet shallow cracks criss-cross the ice
How did they come to be?

Io is erupting
Volcanos rising high
The "tidal pump" of Jupiter
Brings sulfur to the sky!

Four of the moons of Jupiter
With mysteries galore,
If four are not enough for you
There are at least twelve more!

Background for Teachers

Copernicus's Theory

The idea that the Earth travels around the Sun was suggested in ancient Greece, by Aristarchus in the 3rd century B.C. There's a crater on our Moon that is named after him. However, it was Copernicus, in the 16th century, who came up with the first detailed mathematical theory postulating that the Earth is not the center of the Universe.

We hear so much about how the Roman Catholic Church persecuted Galileo for teaching about and defending the Copernican theory that we may forget that Copernicus was himself serving the Church when he proposed it. He had been asked by the Pope to improve the calendar so the date of Easter could be set more accurately. He found that the best way to do so was to reject Ptolemy's theory, which had been taught as the truth for 1,200 years.

Ptolemy's theory was based on the idea that all celestial bodies circled the Earth. The stars were thought to be attached to a celestial sphere that turned around the Earth once a day. The planets were thought to be nested inside transparent crystal spheres, one inside the other, turning in perfect, intricate circles, so that they moved against the background stars in predictable ways.

One problem with Ptolemy's model was that celestial movements could not be predicted exactly. That was why other astronomers, including Copernicus, came up with alternative models—to try to predict the movements of the planets more precisely. This was important for improving the calendar, as mentioned above, and also for astrology, which was widely practiced at that time.

Copernicus knew that his theory would cause a great stir, so he waited to publish it until he was on his deathbed, in 1543. Later that century a Danish astronomer, Tycho Brahe, invented a number of instruments for measuring the positions of the planets very precisely. His instruments were also able to measure the positions of comets when they chanced to appear in the sky. Tycho observed that a certain comet moved from the distant reaches of the solar system, through the spheres of the planets, and then back toward the stars. If there were crystal spheres that carried the planets, then they must surely be pierced and shattered by Tycho's comet!

Tycho's discovery showed that Ptolemy's theory could not be correct; however, on the other hand, he could not accept Copernicus's idea that the Earth **moved**. So, Tycho Brahe invented his own theory of the solar system. He proposed that

MERCURY
no moons

VENUS
no moons

EARTH
1 moon

MARS
2 moons

ASTEROID BELT

JUPITER
16 moons

SATURN
17 moons

URANUS
15 moons

NEPTUNE
8 moons

PLUTO
1 moon

System of Ptolemy

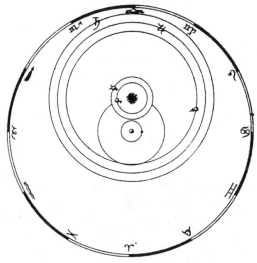

System of Tycho Brahe

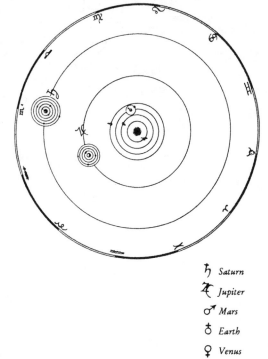

System of Copernicus

♄ *Saturn*

♃ *Jupiter*

♂ *Mars*

♁ *Earth*

♀ *Venus*

☿ *Mercury*

☾ *The Moon (Luna)*

the Earth was indeed the immovable center of the Universe, and that the Sun and Moon went around the Earth. Like Copernicus, however, Tycho's model had all the *other* planets orbiting the Sun.

Galileo, Kepler, and Science Fiction

Tycho Brahe hired an assistant named Johannes Kepler to analyze his measurements to calculate the orbit of Mars. Since they had no calculators in those days, it took Kepler many years to do it. As a result, Kepler was the first to discover that planets move in ellipses (elongated circles), with the Sun at one focus of the ellipse. That added further support to the theory that the Sun, and not the Earth, was the center of the Universe.

Kepler lived at the same time as Galileo, and the two scientists communicated by mail. Kepler was very excited by Galileo's discoveries of the craters and mountains of our Moon. In fact, he became so excited that he wrote the first science fiction story, imagining that perhaps people lived on the Moon! He wrote to Galileo several times, asking for a telescope so that he could see the Moon and the satellites of Jupiter for himself. Unfortunately, Kepler never received his telescope.

As mentioned in Activity 1, Galileo's discovery that Jupiter was circled by four moons helped to persuade many people that the Sun was the center of the Universe, and that the Earth is actually spinning on its axis, and revolving around the Sun once a year, just like the other planets. However, it was not until the early 20th century that telescopes improved enough for astronomers to realize that not even the Sun was the center of the Universe; but that our star is just one of billions in the Milky Way Galaxy, which in turn is just one of billions of galaxies in a vast, expanding universe.

The Moon: A Chip Off the Old Block?

We call it "**the** Moon," but the word "moon" can mean any planetary satellite—a body circling a planet. The name *Luna*, drawn from Roman mythology, identifies our own satellite, just as the names *Callisto* and *Ganymede* identify the two largest satellites of Jupiter.

A wide variety of theories have been proposed to explain the origin of our Moon. As new evidence accumulates from more direct experience, new theories emerge. Several leading theories were rejected when astronauts were able to go there and bring back Moon rocks. For example, the same trace elements appear in both lunar and Earth rocks. That rules out the theory that the our Moon was formed in a different part of the solar system and was captured when it wandered too close to the Earth. On the other hand, there are significant differences between the composition of the Moon and of Earth. The Moon has a much lower density than Earth, and has much less water and iron.

The most widely-held modern view about the origin of the Moon was proposed by William Hartman and Donald Davis in 1974. Their theory is that the early Earth was struck by a Mars-size object, some four billion years ago. The collision blew much of the Earth's mantle into space. Some of it escaped altogether. Some fell back to Earth. And some of it went into orbit around Earth, forming a "ring," much like the "ring" of Saturn. After a few hundred million years, the clumps of rock that made up the "ring" were gradually attracted together by mutual gravity, and formed our familiar Luna. Initially, this theory holds, Luna was much closer to Earth, but over the millennia, it has gradually spiraled outwards to its current position. It is still spiraling outward, ever so slowly. This theory is widely believed to be true because it is consistent with all of the analyses of Moon rocks—but it is unlikely we will ever know *for certain* how the Moon was formed.

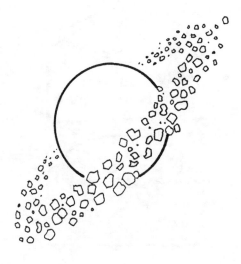

Since the Moon has no atmosphere to protect it, meteors impact it with full size and force. The craters thus formed are not eroded by wind or water; but only by other meteors that strike at a later time. Consequently, it has been possible to date various parts of the Moon's surface by counting the number of craters per square mile. The highlands have the largest number of craters, while the lava-filled dark *maria* have fewer craters. The youngest maria have the fewest craters.

Because of the constant pounding of meteors, the entire surface of the Moon is covered with a thick layer of dust and rock fragments called *regolith*. The maria are covered with regolith layers 2 to 8 meters thick; in the older highlands, these layers are as much as 15 meters thick.

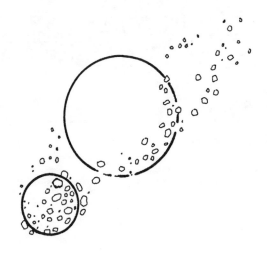

More on Craters

The formation of impact craters on the Moon, as investigated by the cratering activities in this guide, has been fairly well established by laboratory experiments with high speed impacts, and the collection and analysis of lunar rocks. The evidence is quite conclusive that meteors explode on impact.

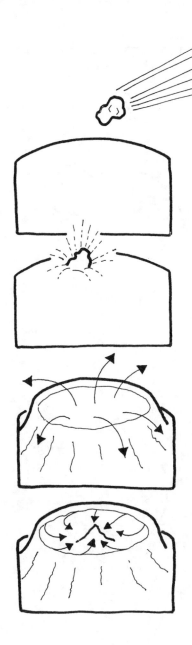

The heat is so intense that the lunar surface at the impact site is turned to liquid, forming a crater basin about twenty times the diameter of the incoming meteor, and forming a mountainous rim. For larger craters, as the rim partially collapses, the liquefied material rebounds into the center, sometimes forming a mountain in the middle of the crater basin. All this takes only a few minutes! Since the gravity of a moon is low, the debris from the explosion settles slowly, and it may be hours before the rays of material blasted from the crater reach out for hundreds of miles across the lunar surface.

The first crater experiments were performed just a few decades after Galileo initially observed the Moon with a telescope. Robert Hooke experimented by boiling a pot of wet plaster which he thought might have represented the Moon when it was first forming. He found that "the whole surface, especially that where some of the last bubbles have risen, will appear all over covered with small pits, exactly shaped like those of the Moon..." Hooke also experimented by throwing bullets and mud pellets into other surfaces and found that they also left marks like craters. However, he did not believe that the craters formed this way, because he did not know that there were any rocks floating around in space. About two hundred years later a very large "shower" of meteors was observed and some of the meteorites were recovered. Finally, people believed that there were rocks in space, and the idea that the Moon's craters were formed by very large meteors was seriously considered.

Studies of the real Moon show that nearly all craters are very nearly circular. Modern experiments also indicate that when high speed meteors strike, they all seem to form circular craters, regardless of the shape of the meteor, and no matter at what angle they strike the surface of the model. This is because the meteor explodes on impact, and the force of the explosion is equal in all directions.

Jupiter: Almost a Star

The Jupiter System has turned out to be a very good analogue to the solar system in more ways than Galileo had anticipated. The two outer satellites, Callisto and Ganymede, are less dense, and therefore contain a higher proportion of water than the inner moons, Europa and Io. A similar pattern is observed when we look at the solar system as a whole. The inner planets, Mercury, Venus, Earth, and Mars, are more dense than the outer planets, from Jupiter to Neptune, which are known as the "gas giants." Pluto is the "oddball." It is denser than the gas giants. It has a large moon, and has a very

© ©

1993: Jan. 22 a

elliptical orbit. It is likely to be a comet-like body in orbit around the Sun.

In the solar system as a whole, it is believed that the inner planets lost their gases because they were blown away by the solar wind. This storm of particles, which began when the Sun ignited as a star, continues to be ejected by the Sun. Currently, the Earth's magnetic field protects us from the solar wind, but in the very early days of the solar system, when Earth was no more than billions of rock fragments that had not yet formed into a large body, the solar wind was unchallenged and very powerful this close to the Sun. The gas giants retained their gases because the solar wind was much weaker in the outer reaches of the solar system. Today, most of the planets are protected from the solar wind by their own magnetic fields.

A similar situation seemed to exist near Jupiter. If Jupiter had been a little more massive, it is possible that its nuclear fires would have ignited, and it would have become a star. In that case, the Sun would have been part of a very close binary star system, and the Earth would not have enjoyed a stable environment, conducive to the evolution of life. Still, Jupiter was very hot in its early years. As gravity pulled in matter into a smaller and smaller volume, its temperature increased. The effects of the satellites themselves, creating huge tides on Jupiter's gaseous body, may have caused further heating. The heat energy from Jupiter would have driven off water and other gases from the closest bodies, Io and Europa, while the more distant Callisto and Ganymede retained their complement of about 50% water.

Eventually, three of the four Galilean moons cooled off and formed icy surfaces. But not Io. Being so close to massive Jupiter, it is constantly being squeezed by tidal and magnetic forces, causing its interior to heat up. The molten interior results in volcanoes which spew forth sulfurous compounds into space. A ring, or *torus*, of solid and gaseous particles now circles Jupiter, keeping Io company in its orbit. These particles come from Io's volcanoes.

The Red Spot

No discussion of the "Giant Planet" is complete without some mention of the Great Red Spot. Even though it is now thought to be a storm system, telescopic observations show that it has been in existence at least 300 years. Can you imagine a hurricane on Earth lasting for that long?

Also remarkable is the size of the Great Red Spot. About three Earths could fit into it neatly. The red spot is embedded in one of several zones of moving cloud bands that stripe the planet. Close-up photos taken by the Voyager spacecraft also show a wide variety of other circular cloud systems and incredibly detailed eddy currents.

Despite 300 years of observations, detailed photos, and a host of computer studies, scientists are still not certain what caused the Red Spot to form and what keeps it going. One theory is that it is driven by heat from below; another that it is caused by the interaction of two adjacent atmospheric zones moving at different speeds; a third is that it absorbs energy from smaller storms. The Great Red Spot remains a mystery for one of your students to figure out.

The Inner Moons and Ring

You may want to explain to your students that Amalthea is not actually ball-shaped like the larger moons of Jupiter. A very blurry photograph taken by the Voyager 1 spacecraft shows that Amalthea is reddish in color and shaped like a very irregular strawberry, about 135 km long, and only about 75 km wide. Some of the other small moons of Jupiter are also irregular in shape.

The four inner moons, Metis, Adrastea, Amalthea, and Thebe, are so close to Jupiter (the closest is only 1.8 radii from the center of the planet) that it is unlikely that they could have been there since the formation of the solar system. They were probably captured by Jupiter's strong gravity, or are fragments of larger bodies that collided with other moons.

The four inner moons are embedded in a ring of rock fragments. Jupiter's ring is so tenuous that it was not observed until Voyager 2 looked back after passing Jupiter, in the direction of the Sun. The Sun's light was reflected by the material in the rings, as dust in the air is sometimes reflected in a ray of sunlight.

Over millions of years, the rock fragments collide and are broken into tinier bits. Eventually, they spiral down into the planet's atmosphere. So, in order for the ring to exist at all, it must be replenished, probably by collisions between the existing moons.

The Outer Moons

Jupiter's eight most-distant moons are called "irregular" because they do not orbit in the same plane that Jupiter and all of the other planets (except Pluto) orbit the Sun. Their orbits are inclined to the plane (called the *ecliptic*) by from 30° to 163°. In contrast, our own Luna orbits very close to the plane of the ecliptic, inclined from it by only 5°.

Four of these moons, Elara, Lysithea, Himalia, and Leda, are about 160 Jupiter radii from its center. They orbit in the same direction as the four Galilean moons (clockwise as

1993: Jan. 22 b

observed from above Jupiter's north pole). The four outermost moons, Sinope, Pasiphae, Carme, and Ananke, orbit in the opposite direction. The unusual orbital direction and the angle that these moons make to the ecliptic make it very likely that they were captured by Jupiter's gravity, possibly from the asteroid belt.

The Galileo Mission

One more unmanned mission is on its way to Jupiter. The Galileo probe is scheduled to reach the Jupiter system in 1995, where it will drop a package of instruments into the clouds of Jupiter itself, and then make a series of looping orbits of the planet, taking close-up photos of the moons. It is scheduled to pass so close to Io that it will be able to image objects as small as 66 feet across. So stay tuned, the unimaginably huge and ever-fascinating Jupiter System may have more surprises in store for us yet!

Like Galileo

Like Galileo we can see,
Near planet of great mystery,
These bright and circling lights.
We trace the orbits of these orbs,
Ellipses of these satellites.

Near giant of our solar clan,
The moons of Jupiter emerge—
Shine out to us across huge span.
Against a vast and orange expanse,
With gravity, these moons do dance. ●

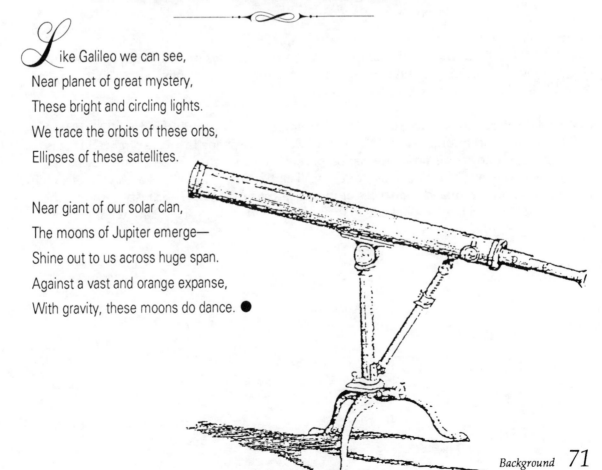

Background 71

TEACHER RESOURCES

NASA, Teacher Resource Centers. Educational materials include videos and slides on the Voyager and other missions. Materials can be ordered from your nearest local NASA Teacher Resource Center listed on page 59 of this guide. For information on *NASA Classroom Activities and Information Sheets* (NASA CORE volume) as well as *Activities in Planetary Geology*, see your local center.

Jet Propulsion Laboratory Teacher Resource Center, JPL Educational Outreach, Mail Stop CS-530, Pasadena, CA 91109. Phone: (818) 354-6916. Specializes in inquiries related to space and planetary exploration, and other JPL activities.

Astronomical Society of the Pacific, 390 Ashton Ave., San Francisco, CA 94112. A nonprofit, international society that serves as a resource for scientists, teachers, students and astronomy enthusiasts. Educational materials include the Astronomy Catalog of slides, software, videos, posters and more, *The Universe In the Classroom*, a newsletter on teaching astronomy (grades 3 - 12) and *Mercury* magazine, the Society journal.

Association of Lunar and Planetary Observers (ALPO). c/o John E. Westfall, P.O. Box 16131, San Francisco, CA 94116. An international organization for amateur and professional astronomers. A special group of observers draw and photograph Jupiter and its moons, time special events and watch for unusual occurrences. Teachers and students may write for information on available materials (e.g., charts, instructional handbooks, observational report forms), for the quarterly journal, or for information on workshops and conventions.

British Astronomical Association. Burlington House, Piccadilly, London, England W1V9AG. Teachers and students are invited to write this international organization of astronomers for information about this association, which publishes sky charts, a journal, and education materials for observers.

Space Telescope Science Institute. 3700 San Martin Drive, Baltimore, MD 21218. The Education and Public Affairs Office at the Space Telescope Institute offers slide sets, posters, photographs and information packets which include recent Hubble Space Telescope views of Jupiter. "Astronomy Visualization" videotapes are available, including dramatic animated sequences of Jupiter and its moons. S.T.Sc.I. sponsors teacher workshops and makes available to the public a wide range of educational materials.

© ©
1993: Jan. 23 a

Computer Software Resources

Voyager (for the Macintosh)
The Interactive Desktop Planetarium
Carina Software
830 Williams Street
San Leandro, CA 94577
(510) 352-7328

Dance of the Planets (IBM compatible)
ARC Science Simulations
PO Box 1955S
Loveland, CO 80539

The Sky: Astronomy Software (for Windows)
Software Bisque
912 Twelfth Street, Suite A
Golden, CO 80401
1-800-843-7599

ORBITS (IBM and compatible)
Software Marketing Corporation
98312 S. 51st Street, C-113
Phoenix, AZ 85044

Distant Suns
(Macintosh and Windows versions)
Virtual Reality Laboratories
2341 Ganador Court
San Luis Obispo, CA 93401-9826

Night Sky (IBM compatible)
Zephyr Services
1900 Murray Avenue, Dept. A
Pittsburgh, PA 15217
1-800-533-6666

Astronomy Lab (IBM)
Zephyr Services
1900 Murray Avenue, Dept. A
Pittsburgh, PA 15217
1-800-533-6666

The Planetary Construction Set (Apple II)
Sunburst Communications
P. O. Box 40
39 Washington Avenue
Pleasantville, NY 10570
(800) 321-7511

Special thanks to John Hewitt
of the Astronomy/Physics department at the
Lawrence Hall of Science
for his help with this list.

RECOMMENDED READING
(Many of these references and reviews were provided by the
Astronomical Society of the Pacific, Teachers Resource Notebook)

Reference Books

Beatty, J. & Chaikin, A., *The New Solar System*, 3rd ed. 1990, Sky Publishing, Cambridge. Beautifully illustrated with articles on all aspects of planetary astronomy.

Bishop, R., ed. Royal Astronomical Society of Canada, *Observer's Handbook*, 136 Dupont Street, Toronto, Ontario M5R 1V2. An annual guide to celestial events and cycles.

Menzel, D. & Pasachoff, J. *A Field Guide to the Stars and Planets*, 2nd ed. 1983, Houghton-Mifflin paperback. Updated edition of a classic guide full of information and maps.

Moore, P. *Exploring the Night Sky with Binoculars*. 1986, Cambridge University Press. Clear and simple introduction to the subject.

Morrison, D. & Samz, J. *Voyage to Jupiter*. 1980, NASA SP - 439. Best introduction.

Whitney, C. *Whitney's Star Finder*, 5th ed. 1990, Random House paperbound. Basic primer on constellations and sky phenomena. (Updated periodically)

Yeates, C., et al. *Galileo: Exploration of Jupiter's System*. 1985, NASA Special Publication SP - 479.

Yenne, B. & Garratte, S., ed. *To The Edge of The Universe, The Exploration of Outer Space With NASA*. 1986, Exeter Books, Bookthrift Marketing Inc., New York. What we have learned since astronomy began and mysteries that remain to be solved.

For Students (and Teachers, too!)

Colonizing the Planets and Stars, Isaac Asimov, Grade level: 4-6. Explores the possibility of establishing colonies in space, traveling by starship to other galaxies, and meeting extraterrestrials. NASA photos and color illustrations. (1990)

Comets and Meteors, Isaac Asimov, Grade level 4-6. History and observations of meteors and comets. Includes Halley's Comet, a Fact File and resource section. Color pictures and illustrations. (1990)

Galileo, Leonard Everett Fisher, Grade level 4-7. An excellent and accessible young people's biography of Galileo. (1992)

Jupiter, Seymour Simon, William Morrow & Company, New York. Grade level: 4-7. A close-up look at this strange and mysterious planet through full-color photographs. (1985)

Meteors and Meteorites - Voyagers from Space, Patricia Lauber, Thomas Y. Crowell Jr. Books, New York. Grade level: 7-9. Explores current scientific thinking about meteorites as clues to the origin of the solar system, and about violent collisions with comets and space rocks. NASA photos, pictures and drawing. (1989)

Seeing Earth From Space, Patricia Lauber, Orchard Books, New York. Grade level: 7 and up for reading, illustrations for all ages. Beautiful and intriguing photographs of space-ship Earth. Focuses on what can be learned by studying images formed from data collected by satellites.

Space Library: Space Walking, Gregory Vogt, Franklin Watts, New York. Grade level: 10-12. A description of human beings' ability to survive in space. Explains space suits, space and moon walks, space stations, and future projects in space. NASA photos of space walks in space and on the Moon. (1987)

The Golden Book of Stars and Planets, Judith Herbst, Western Publishing Co. Inc., Racine, Wisconsin. Grade level: 4-6. Basic introduction to the origins of astronomy, the solar system, descriptions of planets' sizes, atmospheres, environments, plus comets, meteors, etc. NASA photos and color illustrations. (1988)

The Planets - The Next Frontier, David J. Darling, Grade level: 5-9. Describes our solar system, and what we know of each planet from spacecraft. Includes Voyager's discoveries in the systems of Jupiter and Saturn. Color illustrations. (1985)

Voyager, Missions in Space, Gregory Voyt, The Millbrook Press, Brookfield, Connecticut. Grade level: 7-10. "Inside-look" at the missions of Voyager 1 and 2. Includes beautiful NASA images of the Gas Giants, their satellites and deep space. (1991)

Voyager To The Planets, Necia Apfel, Clarion Books, New York. Grade level: 6-8. A dramatic story of the Voyager mission including data and photographs received from the spacecraft during its continuing journey. (1991)

Magazines and Newsletters

Abrams Planetarium Sky Calendar. Available free with membership in the Astronomical Society of the Pacific (see above organizations) or from Abrams Planetarium, Michigan State University, East Lansing, MI 48824. Concise one-page monthly sky calendar and simple star chart tells you what to look for and where each month.

Astronomy. Kalmbach Publishing, P.O. Box 1612, Waukesha, WI 53187. Monthly magazine for beginners and other astronomy enthusiasts.

Odyssey. Cobblestone Publishing Inc., 30 Grove Street, Peterborough, NH 03458. (603/924-7209). Monthly magazine that includes basic astronomy, word games and puzzles for young astronomers. (Ages 8–14 years, published 10 times per year.)

Sky & Telescope. Sky Publishing, P.O. Box 9111, Belmont MA 02178. Monthly magazine with articles written by and for the professional and amateur astronomer.

The Universe In the Classroom: A Newsletter on Teaching Astronomy. Astronomical Society of the Pacific, Teacher's Newsletter, Dept. N, 390 Ashton Ave. San Francisco, CA 94112. (Please write on *school stationary* and indicate grade level to be included on the mailing list.) A free classroom resource for grades 3–12.

STARnews. Project STAR, Center for Astrophysics, 60 Garden St., Cambridge, MA 02138. A quarterly newsletter specializing in teaching astronomy at the secondary level.

Astronomy Day Handbook. Published by The Astronomical League for organizations wishing to plan special Astronomy Day events. Includes ideas for special events and activities, and gives over 200 addresses for astronomical organizations and sources for educational materials, including space camps, scholarships, teacher training courses and publications for classroom teachers. Contact Gary Tomlinson, Astronomy Day Coordinator, Public Museum of Grand Rapids, 54 Jefferson S.E., Grand Rapids, MI 49503. (616) 456-3987.

Articles

Elliott, J., Kerr, R. "How Jupiter's Ring Was Discovered" in *Mercury*, November/December 1985, page 162.

Gingerich, Owen. "How Galileo Changed the Rules of Science" in *Sky & Telescope*, March 1993, pages 32–36.

Gore, R. "Voyager Views Jupiter" in *National Geographic*, January 1980.

Hartmann, W. "The View from Io" in *Astronomy*, May 1981, page 17.

Johnson, T., Soderblum L. "Io" in *Scientific American*, December 1983.

Morrison, D. "An Enigma Called Io" in *Sky & Telescope*, March 1985, page 198.

Morrison, D. "Four New Worlds: The Voyager Exploration of Jupiter's Satellites" in *Mercury*, May/June 1980, page 53.

Simon, S. "The View from Europa" in *Astronomy*, November 1986, page 98.

Soderblom, L. "The Galilean Moons of Jupiter" in *Scientific American*, January 1980.

LITERATURE CONNECTIONS

Science fiction provides many fine literary connections and extensions for this GEMS guide. The play by Brecht gives students dramatic insight into Galileo's life, and even contains information on his observations—the same observations the students make via slides in the classroom. Other books about Galileo or about telescopic observation also make good connections.

Several of the books involve exploring and colonizing other planets. In *The Planets* there is a highly sophisticated science fiction story about colonization of one of Jupiter's moons. Look for any good stories about exploration and settlement of the Earth's Moon, or other planets/galaxies. Ethical issues are often involved, including: nationalistic competition on Earth in the "race for space," imagined diplomatic and/or antagonistic relations with extraterrestrials, and whether or not to colonize or exploit natural resources found in space.

Venus, Mars, and Jupiter, because of their prominence in the nighttime sky, have inspired a large number of folktales, legends, and myths. Their rising and setting times are often important agricultural markers. Books such as *Star Tales: North American Indian Stories* or *They Dance in the Sky* are but two examples from many that provide great opportunities for literary connections and increased cultural understandings.

2010: Odyssey Two
by Arthur C. Clarke
Ballantine Books, New York. 1982
Grades: 10–Adult

> This complex, mysterious, and thought-provoking sequel to Clarke's *2001: A Space Odyssey* had the benefit of being written subsequent to the Voyager mission. Chapter 13 specifically, "The Worlds of Galileo," focuses on the four main moons of Jupiter, although there are fascinating observations, accurate scientific information, and lots of interesting speculation about Jupiter and its moons throughout the book, not to mention spirits of intergalactic intelligence and Jupiter becoming a second sun. More advanced students may want to evaluate the accuracy of Clarke's descriptions of Io, Europa, Ganymede, and Callisto.

Against Infinity
by Gregory Benford
Simon and Shuster, New York. 1983
Grades 10–Adult

> This science fiction novel is an account of human settlement on Jupiter's largest moon, Ganymede. The story takes place several hundred years into the colonization process, and begins from the perspective of a 13-year-old boy whose father is one of the leaders of the settlement. The novel ties in well with the final session in which student teams undertake scientific missions to devise and build moon settlements on one of Jupiter's moons. Advanced students may want to read this novel to gather ideas about constructing biospheres, melting ice, obtaining minerals, and other ways humans might possibly survive on the moons of Jupiter. (The author is a Professor of Physics at the University of California, Irvine.)

Einstein Anderson Makes Up for Lost Time

by Seymour Simon; illustrated by Fred Winkowski
Viking Penguin, New York. 1981
Grades: 4–7

> Chapter 6 poses the question "How can Einstein tell a planet from a star without using a telescope?" He explains to his friend Dennis that although stars twinkle, planets usually shine with a steady light. Looking through the telescope, he thinks the steady light he sees is Jupiter. The four faint points of steady light nearby are Jupiter's moons.

Galileo

by Leonard Everett Fisher
Macmillan Publishing, New York. 1992
Grades 3–7

> This non-fiction work provides a carefully written and well-illustrated account of Galileo's life and accomplishments. His observations of Jupiter's moons are placed in the context of a life of remarkable discoveries in many fields. The book handles the conflict with the Catholic Church in an interesting and balanced way, including modern Papal statements in a brief "More About Galileo" section at the end of the book. An excellent way to provide students with a concise assessment of Galileo's many accomplishments, triumphs, and tragedies.

The Jupiter Theft

by Donald Moffitt
Ballantine Books, New York. 1977
Grades 7–Adult

> Strange, advanced beings from somewhere near the constellation of Cygnus encounter a Jupiter expedition from Earth. The Cygnans want to take Jupiter away to use as a power source as they migrate through the universe. There is some graphic violence as various life forms attack and/or ally with each other, but in general the focus is on scientific speculation. In addition to interesting descriptions of Jupiter and its moons, the book has a wealth of cogent speculation on the possibilities and varieties of life on other worlds.

Jupiter Project

by Gregory Benford
Bantam Books, New York. 1990
Grades 7–10

> A teenager lives with his family as part of a large scientific laboratory that orbits Jupiter, but he is ordered to return home. He has one chance to stay—if he can make an important discovery. There is a nice mix of physics and astronomy with teen-age rebellion and growing maturity, some love interest, and an exciting plot. The descriptions in Chapters 6, 7, and 8, which are part of an account of an expedition to Ganymede, could be compared by students to the information they observe and learn about this mammoth moon.

Life of Galileo
by Bertolt Brecht
Grove Weidenfeld, New York. 1966
Grades 9–12

> This play is a rich literary extension to this unit. During the early scenes of the play, there are several references to, explanations of, and controversies about the telescope, Galileo's observations of the Earth's moon *Luna*, and the implications of his tracking of Jupiter's moons—the exact activity that the students recreate during the first activity. Much of the rest of the play focuses on science and society, church policies of the time, and other incisive social criticism characteristic of Brecht. Dramatizing several of the early scenes would make a great extension, and Galileo's long speech near the end of the play raises relevant issues. (The play is also available in the collection *Brecht: Collected Plays*, Vintage Books, Random House, 1972.)

Star Tales: North American Indian Stories
retold and illustrated by Gretchen W. Mayo
Walker & Co., New York, 1987
Grades: 5–12

> The nine legends in this collection explain observations of the stars, moon, and night sky. Accompanying each tale is information about the constellation or other heavenly observation and how various peoples perceived and interpreted it.

The Faces of CETI
by Mary Caraker
Houghton Mifflin, Boston. 1991
Grades: 6–12

> In this science fiction thriller, colonists from Earth form two settlements on adjoining planets of the Tau Ceti system. One colony tries to survive by dominating the natural forces that they encounter, while those who land on the planet Ceti apply sound ecological principles and strive to live harmoniously in their new environment. Nonetheless, the Cetians encounter a terrible dilemma—the only edible food on the planet appears to be a species of native animals called the Hlur. Two teen-age colonists risk their lives in a desperate effort to save their fellow colonists from starvation without killing the gentle Hlur.

The Planets
edited by Byron Preiss
Bantam Books, New York. 1985
Grades: 8–Adult

This extremely rich, high-quality anthology pairs a non-fiction essay with a fictional work about the earth, moon, each of the planets, and asteroids and comets. Introductory essays are by Isaac Asimov, Arthur C. Clarke and others. The material is dazzlingly illustrated with color photographs from the archives of NASA and the Jet Propulsion Laboratory, and paintings by astronomical artists such as the movie production designers of *2001* and *Star Wars*. "The Future of the Jovian System" by Gregory Benford (about colonization and development of Jupiter's moon Ganymede) is a perfect match to the final activity. However, since the vocabulary is sophisticated it may be more suitable for high-level readers.

The Three Astronauts
by Umberto Eco; illustrated by Eugenio Carmi
Harcourt Brace Jovanovich, San Diego. 1989
Grades: K–5

An American, a Russian, and a Chinese astronaut take off separately in their own rockets with the goal of being first on Mars. They all land at the same time, immediately distrusting each other. When they encounter a Martian their cultural differences disappear as they unite against him. In a surprise happy ending, they recognize the humanity of the Martian after observing his charity toward a baby bird and extend this understanding to differences between all peoples. Younger children may not get the full benefit of the sophisticated illustrations and humor. The astronauts are all male, with no women characters or references.

They Dance in the Sky: Native American Star Myths
by Jean Guard Monroe and Ray A. Williamson
Houghton Mifflin Boston. 1987
Grades 2–8

This book, which is great for reading aloud, includes stories from many Native American regions and peoples, including the Southwest and Southeast, the Plains Indians, the Pawnee, the Northwest Coast, and California Indians. Stories about the Pleiades, the Big Dipper, and the "Star Beings" are particularly noteworthy, but all are imaginative and intriguing. Stories like these from Native American and other world cultures can be interwoven with astronomy activities, provide a sense of careful observation over time, and highlight how the stars and planets have always inspired the human imagination.

Summary Outlines

Activity 1: Tracking Jupiter's Moons

Getting Ready
1. Make one copy of data sheet for each student.
2. Plan how to divide the teams.
3. Set up the slide projector, with slides #1–#11.

Galileo and His Telescope
1. Explain that Galileo was the first person to study the sky using a telescope. (He did not invent the telescope.)
2. Ask/discuss what a planet looks like in sky, with/without a telescope, and show first slide.
3. Explain that when Galileo observed Jupiter he saw four points of light that moved. The class will observe these objects over time, just as Galileo did.

Tracking Jupiter's Moons
1. Hand out data sheets and pencils.
2. Explain that the class will watch Jupiter and its moons for nine nights.
3. Advance to "Night 1" slide (numbers equal distance from Jupiter in millions of miles)
Mention that moons are colored to help tell them apart.
4. Divide class into "teams of astronomers." Each team observes one of the moons.
5. Advance slides as described in teacher's guide, checking to make sure students are recording correctly, and asking for predictions.

Summarizing the Data
1. Have students draw a line connecting the positions of their moon.
2. Have them compare data with students who observed the same moon, and allow time for discussion of differences.
3. Ask what might be happening that would explain why the moons seem to change position each night. [The moon is circling the planet.]
4. Model a moon orbiting Jupiter with a small and large ball.
5. Ask for ideas about figuring out how long one orbit takes.
6. Have students work together counting the spaces between the lines to see how many days have gone by since Night #1.
7. Circulate to all teams, assisting as needed, especially those working on the white moon's orbital period.

Discussing the Results
1. Record all of the groups' results on chalkboard or overhead projector.
2. It is not important that student results match scientific figures exactly. Red moon (Io): two days; Yellow moon (Europa): four days; Blue moon (Ganymede): seven days; White moon (Callisto): 16 days.
3. Ask about relationship between moon's distance from planet and orbital period. [the farther away, the more time]

4. Show Slide #11, Galileo's notes, and discuss what they can recognize.
5. Ask for ideas about why Galileo's discovery was so important.
6. Discuss Copernicus and Earth's revolution around the Sun. Galileo's findings about the Jupiter system were also a model for the solar system.

Activity 2: Experimenting with Craters

Getting Ready
1. Collect and sort needed rocks.
2. Make copy of "Craters" data sheet for each student.
3. Assemble materials.
4. Try the activity yourself.
5. Plan how to present introductions away from materials.
6. Set up slide projector, with #12 and #13 ready.

Meteors and Craters
1. Earth's Moon is named Luna. Ask students to imagine landing on its surface.
2. Show Slide #12 and ask what they see on Luna's surface.
3. Ask what could cause craters on the Moon. Discuss meteors.
4. Discuss Earth and its craters.
5. Have students rub hands together and discuss heat of friction that burns up meteors falling through Earth's atmosphere.

Making Craters
1. Class will investigate what happens when a meteor hits a solid surface.
2. Demonstrate the technique.
3. Ask for predictions.
4. Emphasize dropping rocks carefully.

Free Exploration and Meteor Experiments
1. Distribute materials and have students freely explore.
2. Gather students in area away from materials to ask what students found out and explain the procedures for the two experiments: Size of Rock; Speed of Impact.
3. Make sure students understand procedures. Hand out data sheets and paper rulers and have them begin.
4. Circulate to make sure teams are working safely and cooperatively.
5. Clean up.

Discussing the Results
1. Have class describe their findings from Experiments #1 and #2. Does the size of the meteoroid have anything to do with the size of the crater? Does the size of the crater have anything to do with the speed of a meteor?
2. Show the slide of the Earth's Moon and close-up of a Moon crater. Ask students to point out features they recognize from their experiments.

Activity 3: A Scale Model of the Jupiter System

Getting Ready
1. For the Earth-Moon scale model: blow up a blue balloon (or ball) and have two white balloons (or balls) available. Measure a 7.7 meter distance from the Earth balloon to a wall and tape/attach the other moon (or ball) there.
2. For the Jupiter system scale model: use meter stick to measure string and practice making arc on chalkboard. Read through the session and decide on whether or not you will go outside. Choose an outside area that can encompass a distance of 124 feet. Prepare manila folders as described in guide.

Introducing Scale Models
1. Students give examples of scale models.
2. Discuss meaning of "to scale."
3. Students will work as a whole class and use the metric system.

Presenting the Earth-Moon Scale Model
1. Hold up the blue balloon, representing Earth.
2. Explain that 1 cm in model is 500 km.
3. How big would the Moon be in this scale?
4. Make the "moon" orbit the "Earth." How far away should the "moon" be?
5. After their responses, point to the "moon" you taped 7.7 meters from "Earth." Will the "moon's" whole orbit fit into the classroom [No].

The Jupiter Scale Model System
1. In this scale of Earth/moon, how big would Jupiter be?
2. Could show image of Jupiter: 3 Earths in the red spot!
3. Draw Jupiter arc on board; students imagine it as circle. Compare to Earth balloon. If Jupiter were hollow, 1000 Earths could be jammed inside.
4. Which is the moon closest to Jupiter? [Io] Hold up manila folder with Io drawn to scale. Bigger or smaller than Earth's Moon? [slightly bigger] Have a student pace off 8 meters from "Jupiter" to "Io." Hold up folders of three other moons.
5. Will the other moons fit in the classroom? [No]
6. If possible, go outside and pace off distances to all four moons as described in guide.
7. Back in the classroom, explain that planets of Solar System revolve around Sun just as moons around Jupiter do. How far away from Jupiter would Sun be at this scale? [15 kilometers].

Activity 4: "Grand Tour" of the Jupiter System

Getting Ready
1. Copy the two data sheets for each student.
2. Set up slide projector with slides # 14 – # 23. Look at them yourself.

Decide how to partially darken room.
3. Read the Teacher Fact Sheets and the "Background for Teachers" section.

Jupiter's Four Largest Moons
1. Class will now go on imaginary journey to Jupiter system.
2. Hand out data sheets, and explain they are on same scale (1 cm=500 km)
3. Dim the lights and begin "Grand Tour" as described in guide.
4. Share background information and information on teacher fact sheets as appropriate.
5. Tour begins at Callisto then travels inward to other three moons.
6. Students write and draw observations.
7. Help students distinguish evidence from inference.
8. After tour note that students have acted exactly like scientists.

Activity 5: Creating Moon Settlements

Getting Ready
1. Start gathering lots of "doo-dads."
2. Cut posterboard into rectangles.
3. Duplicate "Scientific Mission" data sheets.
4. Assemble each team's supplies.
5. Place materials in accessible location.
6. Arrange desks or tables for groups.

Planning Settlements
1. Students imagine themselves exploring the moons.
2. They will work in teams to build models of settlements.
3. Consider conditions they will face: gravity, temperature, etc.
4. Divide the class into teams and make sure all four moons represented.
5. Each moon settlement has different mission.

Building the Settlement
1. Show class the posterboard base.
2. Emphasize sharing and cooperation.
3. Have students get raw materials, begin planning and building.
4. Bring around labels.
5. Leave enough time for cleaning up.

Discussing Lunar Settlements
1. Plan sufficient time for students to report.
2. Allow time for other students to ask questions.
3. Ask questions as needed to focus discussion.
4. Consider doing several "Going Furthers."

HAVE FUN EXPLORING THE MOONS OF JUPITER!

JUPITER: ORBITAL AND PHYSICAL CHARACTERISTICS

Orbital period[1]: 11.9 years
Rotational period[2]: 9.92 hours
Distance from Sun[3]: 5.20 AU
Diameter at equator: 141,925 kilometers
Diameter at poles: 132,883 kilometers
Mass[4]: (Earth =1) 318
Density[5]: (water = 1) 1.3
Surface Gravity[6]: (Earth =1) 2.54
Inclination of axis: 3.1
Maximum Surface temperature: -180 F
Minimum Surface temperature: -200 F
Number of Satellites: 16+

JUPITER: STRUCTURAL CHARACTERISTICS

Rings: Primary components are charged dust particles. (8% of Jupiter's radius)

Atmosphere: Cloud decks of ammonia, ammonium hydrosulfides, water above molecular hydrogen and helium. (12% of Jupiter's radius)

Mantle: Mostly liquid metallic hydrogen and helium. (68% of Jupiter's radius)

Core: Includes metals, silicates, ices. (20% of Jupiter's radius)

[1] *Orbital Period* is the time it takes the planet to revolve once around the Sun.
[2] *Rotational Period* is the time the planet takes to spin on its axis with reference to the stars.
[3] *Distance from Sun* is given in AU or Astronomical Units. 1 AU is the Earth's average distance from the Sun (149,6000,000 kilometers).
[4] *Mass* is given compared to Earth's mass, which is 5.997 x 1027 grams.
[5] *Density* is given compared to water. The density of water is 1.0 grams per cubic centimeter. The overall density of Jupiter would be 1.3 grams per cubic centimeter.
[6] *Surface Gravity* given is compared to the acceleration gravity produces at the Earth's surface, which is 9.8 meters per second per second.

CHARACTERISTICS OF JUPITER'S SATELLITES

Name of Moon	Year of Discovery	Distance from Jupiter [1] (km)	Orbital Period [2] (days)	Radius [3] (km)
Metis	1979	128,000	0.29	(20)
Adrastea	1979	129,000	0.30	12 x 8
Almalthea	1892	181,000	0.489	135 x 75
Thebe	1979	222,000	0.670	(50)
Io	1610	422,000	1.77	1,816
Europa	1610	671,000	3.55	1,569
Ganymede	1610	1,070,000	7.16	2,631
Callisto	1610	1,883,000	16.7	2,400
Leda	1974	11,100,000	239.0	(8)
Himalia	1904	11,500,000	251.0	(90)
Lysithea	1938	11,720,000	259.0	(20)
Elara	1905	11,740,000	260.0	(40)
Ananke	1951	21,200,000	631.0	(15)
Carme	1938	22,600,000	692.0	(20)
Pasiphae	1908	23,500,000	735.0	(20)
Sinope	1914	23,700,000	758.0	(20)

(Other Satellites are suspected)

Notes and Explanations about the table:

[1]Distance from Jupiter refers to the average distance in kilometers of each satellite from the center (not surface) of its planet.

[2]Orbital Period refers to the time that the satellite takes to revolve around the planet.

[3]Radius is given in kilometers. Values in parentheses are uncertain by more than 10 percent.

Source of Data:
  Beatty, J. K. and Chaikin, A., The New Solar System (Sky Publishing Corporation and Cambridge University Press, 1990)
  Astronomical Society of the Pacific, "The Universe At Your Fingertips, Teachers Resource Notebook"

Notes and Key
for
Jupiter Visibility Chart

You can look for Jupiter as it wanders through our skies on its 12-year journey around the Sun. The approximate sky and horizon directions can be found in the "Jupiter Visibility Chart" on the next page. Down the left side of the chart are the years from 1993 through 2004 and across the top are the months of the year. The chart locates Jupiter in a part of the sky designated by the constellation also seen there at that time, so for example in January 1993 Jupiter appeared in the constellation Virgo. Here is a key to the abbreviations that are used in the chart:

NE, E, SE, S, SW, W, NW = horizon directions (Northeast, East, etc.)

Subscript **L** means low in the sky

Subscript **H** means high in sky

■■■■ means it is not visible

The designation "**a.m.**" indicates that Jupiter, although not visible in the evening sky at that time, can be seen in the early morning hours, just before dawn.

The constellation and Jupiter locations noted in the chart will be most accurate at 9:00 p.m. standard time (± 1 hour), at mid-month, and at 40 degrees North latitude (± 10 degrees latitude).

To find Jupiter with the naked eye, look for the brightest star-like object in the appropriate part of the sky. Using binoculars or a telescope, you may be able to see Jupiter as a disc-shaped object, with one or more bright points of light immediately beside it (the Galilean moons).

For more precise viewing times and locations, please consult a current sky calendar. Monthly sky calendars are often included in astronomy magazines. Sky *& Telescope*, for example, includes viewing and related information on Jupiter and its moons in every issue. See the "Resources for Teachers" section of this guide for other astronomy publications and resources.

JUPITER VISIBILITY CHART

	January	February	March	April	May	June	July	August	September	October	November	December
1993	VIRGO a.m.	VIRGO E_L	VIRGO E	VIRGO SE	VIRGO S	VIRGO SW	VIRGO SW	VIRGO W_L	VIRGO ■	VIRGO ■	VIRGO a.m.	VIRGO a.m.
1994	LIBRA a.m.	LIBRA a.m.	LIBRA a.m.	LIBRA E	LIBRA SE	VIRGO SW	VIRGO SW	LIBRA SW	LIBRA W_L	LIBRA ■	LIBRA ■	LIBRA ■
1995	OPHIUCHUS a.m.	OPHIUCHUS a.m.	OPHIUCHUS a.m.	OPHIUCHUS E_L	OPHIUCHUS E	OPHIUCHUS SE	SCORPIUS S_L	SCORPIUS SW_L	OPHIUCHUS W	OPHIUCHUS ■	OPHIUCHUS ■	OPHIUCHUS ■
1996	SAGITTARIUS ■	SAGITTARIUS a.m.	SAGITTARIUS a.m.	SAGITTARIUS a.m.	SAGITTARIUS a.m.	SAGITTARIUS SE_L	SAGITTARIUS SE_L	SAGITTARIUS S_L	SAGITTARIUS SW_L	SAGITTARIUS W_L	SAGITTARIUS ■	SAGITTARIUS ■
1997	SAGITTARIUS ■	CAPRICORNUS ■	CAPRICORNUS a.m.	CAPRICORNUS a.m.	CAPRICORNUS a.m.	CAPRICORNUS a.m.	CAPRICORNUS E	CAPRICORNUS SE	CAPRICORNUS S	CAPRICORNUS SW	CAPRICORNUS SW_L	CAPRICORNUS ■
1998	CAPRICORNUS ■	AQUARIUS W	AQUARIUS ■	AQUARIUS a.m.	AQUARIUS a.m.	PISCES a.m.	PISCES NE_L	PISCES E	AQUARIUS SE	AQUARIUS S	AQUARIUS SW	AQUARIUS W
1999	PISCES W	PISCES W	CETUS W_L	PISCES a.m.	PISCES a.m.	PISCES a.m.	ARIES a.m.	ARIES NE_L	ARIES E	PISCES SE_H	PISCES S_H	PISCES SW_H
2000	PISCES W	PISCES W	ARIES NW_L	ARIES a.m.	ARIES a.m.	TAURUS a.m.	TAURUS a.m.	TAURUS a.m.	TAURUS a.m.	TAURUS E	TAURUS SE_H	TAURUS SE_H
2001	TAURUS S_H	TAURUS SW_H	TAURUS W_H	TAURUS W_L	TAURUS ■	TAURUS a.m.	GEMINI a.m.	GEMINI a.m.	GEMINI a.m.	GEMINI a.m.	GEMINI NE	GEMINI E
2002	GEMINI SE_H	GEMINI S_H	GEMINI SW_H	GEMINI W	GEMINI W	GEMINI ■	GEMINI ■	CANCER ■	CANCER a.m.	CANCER a.m.	CANCER a.m.	LEO NE_L
2003	CANCER E_H	CANCER SE_H	CANCER S_H	CANCER SW_H	CANCER W_H	CANCER NW_L	LEO NW_L	LEO ■	LEO a.m.	LEO a.m.	LEO a.m.	LEO NE_L
2004	LEO E	LEO SE_H	LEO SE_H	LEO S_H	LEO SW_H	LEO W	LEO NW_L	LEO ■	VIRGO ■	VIRGO ■	VIRGO a.m.	VIRGO a.m.

Number	Slide	Source
1	Jupiter and 4 moons as seen by Galileo	Lawrence Hall of Science
2	Tracking Jupiter's Moons—Night 1	Lawrence Hall of Science
3	Tracking Jupiter's Moons—Night 2	Lawrence Hall of Science
4	Tracking Jupiter's Moons—Night 3	Lawrence Hall of Science
5	Tracking Jupiter's Moons—Night 4	Lawrence Hall of Science
6	Tracking Jupiter's Moons—Night 5	Lawrence Hall of Science
7	Tracking Jupiter's Moons—Night 6	Lawrence Hall of Science
8	Tracking Jupiter's Moons—Night 7	Lawrence Hall of Science
9	Tracking Jupiter's Moons—Night 8	Lawrence Hall of Science
10	Tracking Jupiter's Moons—Night 9	Lawrence Hall of Science
11	Galileo's Notes	Sidereal Messenger, Galilei
12	Earth's Moon, front side, full phase	Hale Observatory
13	Crater, close-up, Earth's Moon	Hale Observatory
14	Jupiter With Two Small Moons	NASA
15	Jupiter's Great Red Spot, Close-Up Comparison with Earth	NASA: composite by Meszaros, Astronomical Society of the Pacific
16	Callisto	NASA
17	Callisto Close-Up	NASA
18	Ganymede	NASA
19	Ganymede Close-Up	NASA
20	Europa	NASA
21	Europa Close-Up	NASA
22	Io	NASA
23	Io Close-Up	NASA

Additional slide sets can be purchased from the: GEMS Project, Lawrence Hall of Science, University of California, Berkeley, CA 94720.

Name _____

Color code
of your moon: _____

TRACKING JUPITER'S MOONS

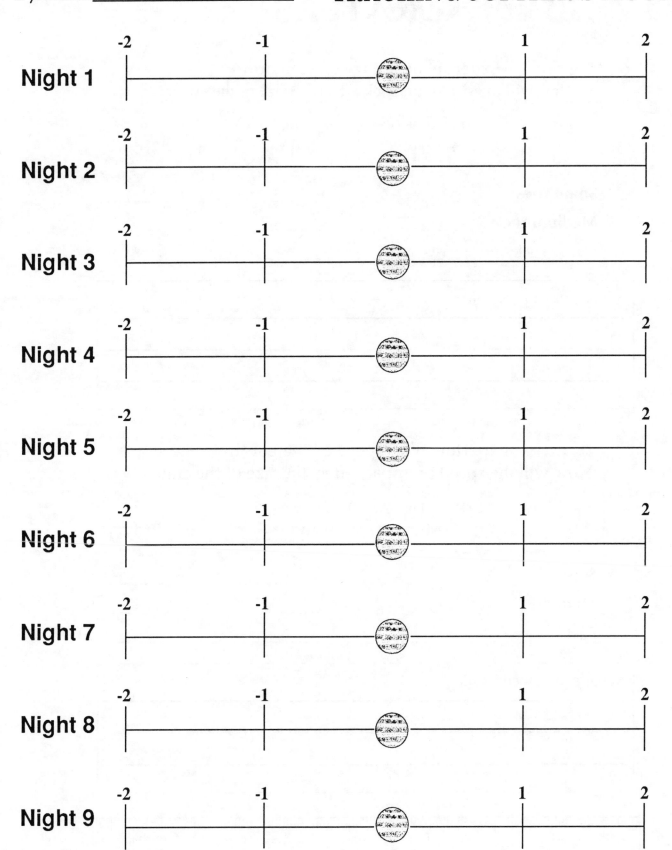

Night 1   -2   -1   1   2

Night 2   -2   -1   1   2

Night 3   -2   -1   1   2

Night 4   -2   -1   1   2

Night 5   -2   -1   1   2

Night 6   -2   -1   1   2

Night 7   -2   -1   1   2

Night 8   -2   -1   1   2

Night 9   -2   -1   1   2

Lawrence Hall of Science
© 1993 by the Regents of the University of California

CRATERS

Experiment 1: Size of Meteoroid
How will the size of the rock affect the size of the crater?

Record the Crater Diameter for:

	1st try	2nd try	3rd try
Small rock	_____	_____	_____
Medium rock	_____	_____	_____
Large rock	_____	_____	_____

What can you conclude?
_____
_____
_____

Experiment 2: Speed of Meteoroid
How will the speed of impact affect the size of the crater?

Record the Crater Diameter for:

	1st try	2nd try	3rd try
Slow	_____	_____	_____
Medium	_____	_____	_____
Fast	_____	_____	_____

What can you conclude?
_____
_____
_____

1 2 3 4 5 6 7 8 9 10 11 12 13 14 15
MM

Lawrence Hall of Science
© 1993 by the Regents of the University of California

MOON MAP

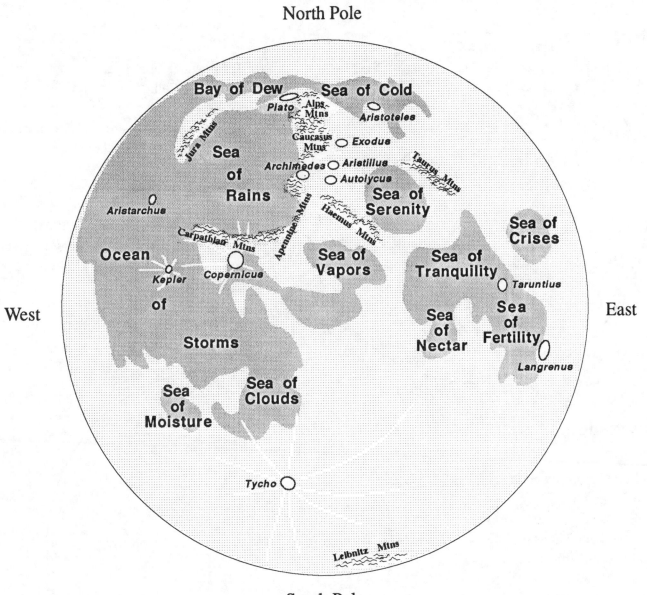

North Pole

Bay of Dew   Sea of Cold

Plato   Alps   *Aristoteles*
          Mtns

Jura Mtns

Sea   *Caucasus*   *Exodus*
of   Mtns
Rains *Archimedes* *Aristillus*   *Taurus Mtns*
              Autolycus

Aristarchus   Sea of
                                 Serenity

                    Apennine Mtns   *Haemus*   Sea of
Carpathian Mtns   Mtns   Crises

Ocean   Copernicus   Sea of   Sea of   Sea of
Kepler   Vapors   Tranquility   Crises

of   *Taruntius*

West   Sea   Sea   East
                                                  of   of
Storms   Sea   Nectar Fertility
                                    of
                                                         Langrenus
Sea   Sea of
of   Clouds
Moisture

Tycho

Leibnitz Mtns

South Pole

Name_____   Date_____

Grand Tour

Callisto

1. Impact craters cover the entire surface of Callisto.

2. The bright spots are probably ice exposed by the impact of large meteors.

3. The largest crater is called **Valhalla**. The bright area is 300 km in diameter, and the largest ring around Valhalla is 3,000 km in diameter.

4. There are no tall mountains and no volcanoes on Callisto.

Ganymede

1. **Galileo Regio** is a dark area, probably very old.

2. Bright impact craters probably reveal ice under the rock.

3. Light brown areas show long ridges of mountains and valleys in close-up views.

Note: Jupiter's moons are drawn to scale. Scale: 1 cm = 500 km

94

Lawrence Hall of Science
© 1993 by the Regents of the University of California

Grand Tour

Europa

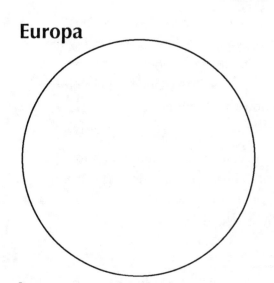

1. The slightly darker region may be a little rougher than the rest of Europa's surface.

2. Fine lines on the surface appear to be cracks, but are not very deep. No one knows for certain what they are.

Io

1. **Pele** is an erupting volcano. The heart-shaped marking is the cloud of material being thrown out by the volcano.

2. **Loki Patera** is a volcano surrounded by a dark lake of liquid sulfur. **Babbar Patera** is another volcano that was erupting when the Voyager Spacecraft flew by.

4. **A close-up view** shows a volcano erupting on the horizon. The material from the volcano is ejecting in a cloud more than 200 kilometers high.

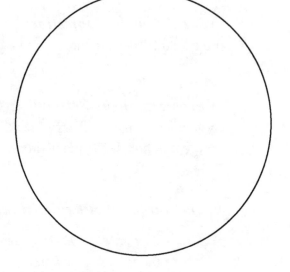

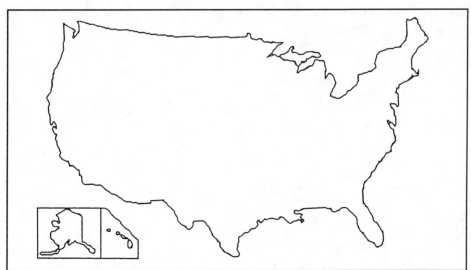

Compare the size of Jupiter's moons to the size of the United States.

All are drawn to scale.
1 cm = 500 km

95

Scientific Mission to Io

Background:

Io is one of the strangest bodies in the solar system. Its volcanoes erupt various compounds of sulfur that have the striking colors of: red, orange, yellow, black, and white. There are about 200 volcanic craters with diameters greater than 20 kilometers. Nine eruptions were recorded by the two Voyager fly-by missions in 1979. Some of the plumes were hundreds of kilometers high. The sulfurous lava flows are hundreds of kilometers long.

There are two theories about why Io has so many volcanoes. One is that it is pushed and pulled by Jupiter's strong gravity, causing it to heat up as it orbits. (This is like the way a paper clip heats up when you bend it back and forth many times.) The other suggests that the heating is caused by Jupiter's strong magnetic field.

Your Scientific Objective: Use an all-terrain electric vehicle to explore volcanoes. Be careful! They are thought to be very hot and may erupt unpredictably.

Your Permanent Settlement Objective: Import water from Europa. Develop a system for using heat energy from the volcanoes to turn the ice into water for drinking, oxygen for breathing, and hydrogen for fuel.

Don't forget about conditions like:

- Low gravity (1/3rd to 1/6th the gravity of Earth)
- Bitter cold temperatures (-100 °C to -200°C), except in lava lake and volcanoes, where temperatures can be well over 70° C (160° F)
- Exposure to cosmic rays and radiation
- No liquid water
- No air
- Little sunlight (1/25th as much as on Earth)

Good Luck!

Lawrence Hall of Science
© 1993 by the Regents of the University of California

Scientific Mission to Europa

Background:

Europa is the most mysterious of Jupiter's satellites. Its surface is one of the smoothest in the solar system. There are no craters larger than 50 kilometers across. This means that Europa may undergo some sort of resurfacing process that may still be occurring. Europa's rocky interior is covered by an icy crust not more than 100 kilometers thick, but possibly as thin as a few hundred meters. There may be an ocean or layer of liquid water, extending as deep as 10 kilometers below the ice. No one knows for certain what the long dark lines are. The large dark areas may be places where Europa has been bombarded by sulfurons material originating from Io.

Your Scientific Objective: Use an all-terrain electric vehicle to explore the dark lines and try to determine their cause. Also drill to determine the depth of ocean and the thickness of surface ice.

Your Permanent Settlement Objective: Establish a system to mine surface ice for export to Io where it will be melted and turned into drinking water, oxygen for breathing, and hydrogen for energy.

Don't forget about conditions like:

- Low gravity (1/3rd to 1/6th the gravity of Earth)
- Bitter cold temperatures (-100 °C to -200°C)
- Exposure to cosmic rays and radiation
- There may be a layer of liquid water below the ice
- No air
- Little sunlight (1/25th as much as on Earth)

Good Luck!

Scientific Mission to Ganymede

Background:

Ganymede is the largest moon in the solar system. The light regions have parallel sets of ridges. They are low mountains, somewhat like the Appalachians on Earth. The dark areas resemble the heavily cratered surface of Callisto and are believed to be older than the light areas.

Your Scientific Objective: Use an all-terrain vehicle to make a survey of the light areas and dark areas to try to determine their origins.

Your Permanent Settlement Objective: Construct a hospital to serve all four moon settlements.

Don't forget about conditions like:

- Low gravity (1/3rd to 1/6th the gravity of Earth)
- Bitter cold temperatures (-100 °C to -200°C)
- Exposure to cosmic rays and radiation
- No liquid water
- No air
- Little sunlight (1/25th as much as on Earth)

Good Luck!

Lawrence Hall of Science
© 1993 by the Regents of the University of California

Scientific Mission to Callisto

Background:

    Callisto has an ice crust of unknown depth. Callisto is almost completely covered with large craters. Most of the craters are believed to be very old — close to 4 billion years. The craters are much flatter than craters formed on rocky moons like Earth's Luna. It is not known whether the flatness of the craters on Callisto is caused by melting of the surface when a meteor strikes, or by the very slow movement of the ice over millions of years.

Your Scientific Objective: Use an all-terrain electric vehicle to make a detailed map of the rings surrounding Valhalla.

Your Permanent Settlement Objective: Make a food production facility that can supply food for all the settlements (less radiation shielding to protect farms would be required on Callisto).

Don't forget about conditions like:

- Low gravity (1/3rd to 1/6th the gravity of Earth)
- Bitter cold temperatures (-100 °C to -200°C)
- Exposure to cosmic rays and radiation (though less radiation than on the other moons)
- No liquid water
- No air
- Little sunlight (1/25th as much as on Earth)

Good Luck!

Lawrence Hall of Science
© 1993 by the Regents of the University of California

Callisto and Ganymede

ⓖ = Ganymede
ⓒ = Callisto

(not to scale)

1. Make up a color code and color the moons in each box according to your code. 2. Cut out the boxes. 3. Tape them onto successive pages of a notepad or book. Be sure each box is positioned in the same orientation and relative location on each page: upper right unbound corner is best. 4. Flip the pages to "run the movie."

1993: Jan. 5 a	1993: Jan. 11 a	1993: Jan. 17 a	1993: Jan. 23 a
1993: Jan. 5 b	1993: Jan. 11 b	1993: Jan. 17 b	1993: Jan. 23 b
1993: Jan. 6 a	1993: Jan. 12 a	1993: Jan. 18 a	1993: Jan. 24 a
1993: Jan. 6 b	1993: Jan. 12 b	1993: Jan. 18 b	1993: Jan. 24 b
1993: Jan. 7 a	1993: Jan. 13 a	1993: Jan. 19 a	1993: Jan. 25 a
1993: Jan. 7 b	1993: Jan. 13 b	1993: Jan. 19 b	1993: Jan. 25 b
1993: Jan. 8 a	1993: Jan. 14 a	1993: Jan. 20 a	1993: Jan. 26 a
1993: Jan. 8 b	1993: Jan. 14 b	1993: Jan. 20 b	1993: Jan. 26 b
1993: Jan. 9 a	1993: Jan. 15 a	1993: Jan. 21 a	1993: Jan. 27 a
1993: Jan. 9 b	1993: Jan. 15 b	1993: Jan. 21 b	1993: Jan. 27 b
1993: Jan. 10 a	1993: Jan. 16 a	1993: Jan. 22 a	1993: Jan. 28 a
1993: Jan. 10 b	1993: Jan. 16 b	1993: Jan. 22 b	1993: Jan. 28 b

GEMS Guides
Please contact GEMS for a descriptive brochure and ordering information

TEACHER'S GUIDES

Acid Rain
Grades 6–10
Animal Defenses
Preschool–K
Animals in Action
Grades 5–9
Bubble Festival
Grades K–6
Bubble-ology
Grades 5–9
Buzzing a Hive
Preschool–3
Chemical Reactions
Grades 6–10
Color Analyzers
Grades 5–8
Convection: A Current Event
Grades 6–9
Crime Lab Chemistry
Grades 4–8
Discovering Density
Grades 6–10
Earth, Moon & Stars
Grades 5–9
Earthworms
Grades 6–10
Experimenting with Model Rockets
Grades 6–10
Fingerprinting
Grades 4–8
Frog Math: Predict, Ponder, Play
Grades K–3
Global Warming
Grades 7–10
Group Solutions
Grades K–4
Height-O-Meters
Grades 6–10
Hide a Butterfly
Preschool–3
Hot Water & Warm Homes from Sunlight
Grades 4–8
In All Probability
Grades 3–6
Investigating Artifacts
Grades K–6
Involving Dissolving
Grades 1–3

Ladybugs
Grades Preschool–1
Liquid Explorations
Grades K–3
Mapping Animal Movements
Grades 5–9
Mapping Fish Habitats
Grades 6–10
Moons of Jupiter
Grades 4–9
More Than Magnifiers
Grades 6–9
Of Cabbages & Chemistry
Grades 4–8
Oobleck: What Do Scientists Do?
Grades 4–8
Paper Towel Testing
Grades 5–8
QUADICE
Grades 4–8
Terrarium Habitats (late 1993)
Grades K–6
Tree Homes
Grades Preschool–1
River Cutters
Grades 6–9
Vitamin C Testing
Grades 4–8

ASSEMBLY PRESENTER'S GUIDES

The "Magic" of Electricity
Grades 3–6
Solids, Liquids, and Gases
Grades 3–6

EXHIBIT GUIDES

Shapes, Loops & Images
all ages
The Wizard's Lab
all ages

HANDBOOKS

GEMS Teacher's Handbook
GEMS Leader's Handbook
A Parent's Guide to GEMS
Once Upon a GEMS Guide
(Literature Connections to GEMS)
To Build a House
(Thematic Approach to Teaching Science)

Write or Call:
GEMS
Lawrence Hall of Science
University of California
Berkeley, CA 94720
(510) 642-7771